The Message Of Aquarius

ANUBIS Collection

The
Message
of
Aquarius

Samael Aun Weor

Gnostic Editions U.K.

Originally published as *El Mensaje de Acuario* by Samael Aun Weor.

© Víctor Manuel Gómez Rodríguez (Samael Aun Weor)
Pseudonym # 2560/91, Book 12, Leaves 154, Mexico D.F.

© Víctor Manuel Gómez Rodríguez
International Registration: El Mensaje de Acuario
No. 11112/91, Book 12, Leaves 398, Mexico D.F.
First published in August 1960, in Bogota, Colombia.

© Gnostic Editions United Kingdom – 2006
Translated by Gnostic Editions U.K.

Published by:
Gnostic Editions U.K.
P.O. Box 53435
London SE18 9BQ

Cover design by Gnostic Editions U.K.

BRITISH LIBRARY CATALOGUING IN PUBLICATION DATA
A catalogue record for this book is available from the British Library.

ISBN: 1-905970-00-5
ISBN: 978-1-905970-00-1 (new format)

Printed and bound in Great Britain by MPG Books Ltd, Bodmin, Cornwall

Contents

Samael Aun Weor

Contemporary esoterist. Founder of the International Gnostic Movement. Author of more than fifty books on Gnostic Esoterism.

Endowed from his childhood with extraordinary faculties of perception which allowed him to gain access to a knowledge that was virtually lost to humanity, but at the same time always present: GNOSIS, or the knowledge of the *ancient initiatory mysteries*.

His mission: To fully revive this knowledge and make it practical and practicable to all men and women of goodwill, regardless of race, creed or social class.

The object of the work of Samael Aun Weor is the *Intimate Self-Realization of the Being*, that is, the complete development of all infinite possibilities that are latent in every human being.

Author's Preface

We call all religions, schools, sects, orders, lodges, etc. to form the World Salvation Army.

We invite all the people of goodwill to join the ranks of the AGLA. We are not against anyone, or against anyone's religion or school.

We consider all religions, schools and sects as precious pearls strung together in the golden thread of the Divinity. We do not attack anyone. We do not hate anyone. We do not combat anyone.

We explain the secret doctrine of our Adorable Saviour.

We love this poor suffering humanity intensely. We warn the Earth's humanity about the apocalyptic hour in which we live.

We remove the veil off the Book of Revelation.

This is a terribly divine book. With this book human beings will have to define themselves as either angels or demons, as either eagles or reptiles.

The times of the end have come and we are in them. Those who suppose the times of the end for a very remote future are very wrong.

Facts speak for themselves. The horrific earthquakes striking Chile recently and causing tremendous damage to Japan; the terrible earthquakes that have happened in different parts of the world; the unknown diseases appearing now everywhere, which medical science cannot cure; the mortal hatred among human beings; the atomic bombs, etc., are all proving to us in an evident way that the times of the end have already come.

Author's Preface

The World Gnostic Movement, the South American Liberating Action and the Sivananda Aryabarta Ashrama are standing up, fighting for the New Aquarian Era. The triangle made up of ALAS, Gnosis and Sivananda Aryabarta Ashrama is fighting for the New Era.

The tremendous hour has come and we cannot remain indifferent.

Soon the atomic war will break out and there will be terrible things in all the corners of the Earth. The apocalyptic hour has come. Woe! woe! woe! to the dwellers of the Earth.

Mexico, 17th August 1960

Introduction

The New Aquarian Era will start on 4th February 1962 between 2 and 3 p.m.

Many schools are awaiting the New Era. This book is the Message of the New Aquarian Era. The announcement of terrifying cataclysms for the Aquarian Era will surprise many esoterist students.

Certainly the I, the myself, the reincarnating ego wants all kinds of comfort. It longs for an era of full security, an era in which all its desires and ambitions will be fulfilled, a comfortable, sensual era, without war, hatred or problems.

It is urgent to know that life has started its return towards the Great Light. This means catastrophe. The Earth will go through a process of planetary disintegration and reintegration. Aquarius brings terrible cataclysms.

Everything that is written in the Book of Revelation is for the times of the end. We have to inform humanity that **the times of the end have already come**.

Revelation is the Message of the New Era. We have studied the apocalyptic verses in the higher worlds.

In this book we state the result of our investigations.

Much has been spoken and written about the Book of Revelation. However, all that has been done is to speculate intellectually and to repeat what supposed authorities have affirmed. That is all.

This work is the result of tremendous esoteric investigations carried out patiently by us in the higher worlds.

Introduction

We have found the Book of Revelation divided into three parts. We have entitled Part One: *The Son of Man*. Part Two is entitled: *The Sealed Scroll*, and the title of Part Three is *The New Jerusalem*.

Part One teaches the Path of the Razor's Edge. Part Two is about the times of the end. Part Three informs us about the future Earth.

This is a book of practical Christification. This is a book of transcendental and absolutely practical Esoterism.

We do not theorize in this book. This is a hundred per cent practical work.

Many students long to become christified, but they do not know where to start. They do not know the key, the secret.

In this book we give the student the key, the secret.

Here you have the key, thirsty lovers of Truth. Now, practise.

You are not alone. We love you deeply. And when you are treading the Path of the Razor's Edge, you will be assisted by us, the Brothers of the Temple.

The AGLA (Amerindia's Liberating Gnostic Action) is made up of the Alas-Gnosis-Sivananda Aryabarta Ashrama triangle.

These are three powerful united movements spreading the Gnostic Esoterism of our Adorable Saviour of the world all over the world.

All those who, after having read this book, want to join the AGLA must write to us. No letter will go unanswered.

The AGLA has millions of people in the West and in the East. The AGLA is the World Salvation Army.

The Supreme Head of the AGLA is the Christ Jesus.

Know Gnostic brothers that **Jesus the Christ is alive**.

The Christ Jesus rose on the third day in his body of flesh and blood, and he is still alive in Shambhala with his same body of flesh and blood.

The secret country of Shambhala is situated in eastern Tibet. There the Master has his own Temple. Many other masters who also rose from the dead and who keep their bodies alive since very ancient ages also live with him there.

The Adorable Master Jesus the Christ has been very active and has worked intensely helping this poor suffering humanity. He is the Head of the Gnostic Movement. He is the Supreme Hierarch of the AGLA.

Unbelievable though it may seem, the Adorable Saviour of the world was working as a male nurse in the battlefields during the first and second world wars.

We are going to transcribe a moving account written by Don Mario Roso de Luna, the illustrious Theosophical writer. This account is found in *The Book That Kills Death* or *Book of the Jinas*, a superb work written by Don Mario. Let us see:

'*We heard strange stories in the trenches. Along the line three hundred miles long stretching from Switzerland down to the sea there were certain rumours, whose origin and truthfulness we did not know. They came and went fast, and I remember the moment when my companion George Casay, looking at me in a strange way with his blue eyes, asked me if I had seen the friend of the wounded, and then he told me what he knew about it. He told me that, after many violent combats, a man dressed in white had been seen leaning over the wounded. Bullets surrounded him; grenades fell around him, but nothing had the power to touch him. He was a hero greater than all heroes, or something still greater. This mysterious personage, whom the French call 'the comrade dressed in white', appeared to be everywhere at the same time: in Nancy, in the Argona, in Soissons, in Ipres; wherever there were men talking about him in a quite voice. Some, nevertheless, smiled saying that trenches made an effect on men's nerves. I, who was often careless in my conversation, exclaimed that in order to believe first I had to see, and that I needed the help of a Germanic knife that caused me to fall wounded on the ground. Next day the events followed one an-*

other very fast in this chunk of the front. Our big guns roared from dawn to nightfall, and they started again the next morning. At midday we were given the order of seizing the trenches opposite to ours. They were two hundred yards away from us, and as soon as we have departed, we realized that our big guns had failed in the preparation. A heart made of steel was needed to keep a man going, but no man hesitated. We had advanced for a hundred and fifty yards when we realized that we were going the wrong way. Our captain ordered us to take cover, and in that precise moment I was wounded in my two legs. By divine mercy I fell into a pit. I suppose that I fainted, because when I opened my eyes, I found myself alone. My pain was horrible, but I did not dare to stir so that the Germans could not see me, since I was fifty yards away from them, and I did not expect them to have pity on me. I felt joyful when it began to get dark. Beside me there were some men who would have considered themselves in danger in the dark, if they had thought that a comrade was still alive. The night fell, and very soon I heard that someone was walking nearby not in a furtive way but in a firm and calm way, as if neither darkness nor death could disturb the calm of those feet. How far I was to suspect who was the one approaching, since although I saw the clarity of what appeared white clothes in the dark, I thought that it was some peasant wearing a shirt, and even it crossed my mind that that person could be an insane woman. But suddenly, with a slight shudder — I do not know if it was from joy or from terror — I then realized that he was the 'comrade dressed in white', and in that very moment the German rifles began to shoot. Hardly could the bullets fail such a target, since he raised his arms as if in supplication, and then he lowered them, remaining in the form of one of those crosses that can be seen so often on the French roadsides. Then he spoke. His words sounded familiar, but all that I remember was the beginning: "Yes, you have known..." And the end: "But now they are hidden from your eyes..."

'Then he leant forward and took me in his arms (I who am the burliest man in my regiment), and carried me as if I was a child.

I suppose that I fell asleep, because when I woke up, this feeling had disappeared. I was a man and I wished to know what I could do for my friend in order to help him and serve him. He was looking towards the stream, and his hands were together, as if in prayer; and then I saw that he was also wounded. I thought I saw something similar to a rent wound in one of his hands, and as he was praying, a drop of blood formed, which fell to the ground. I could not help let out a cry, because that wound seemed to me more horrendous than any wound I had ever seen in this bitter war.

'"You are also wounded," I said timidly. Maybe he heard me, maybe he guessed it from the expression of my countenance; but he answered gently: "That is an old wound, but it has troubled me just recently". And then I noticed in sorrow that the same cruel mark appeared on his foot. You might be surprised that I did not realize it before; I myself was also surprised. But only when I saw his foot I recognized him: THE LIVING CHRIST. I had heard the Chaplain to speak about him a few weeks before, but now I realized that he had come to me (to me who had kept him away from my life in the ardent fever of my youth). I was eager to talk to him and thank him, but I could not find the words. And then he got up and said to me: "Today stay here beside the water. I will come for you tomorrow. I have some work for you so that you can do it for me." Shortly afterwards he left, and while I am waiting for him, I am writing this so that I can remember it later. I feel weak and alone, and my pain increases. But I have his promise. I know that he will come for me tomorrow.'

So far the account given by a soldier and transcribed by Don Mario Roso de Luna in his book *The Book That Kills Death*. This concrete experience proves beyond any doubt that Jesus is still alive with the same physical body he used in the Holy Land.

Here in this book we have given the key to Resurrection. We have torn open the veil of the Sanctuary. We have given the poor suffering humanity the secret doctrine of the Adorable One, with seven seals in the Book of Revelation.

The *Message of Aquarius* is a terribly divine Book of Powers.

All the secrets are here. All the keys to Christification are here.

The Doctrine which the Adorable One taught in secret to his humble disciples is written here.

The Adorable One will remain with us till the end of time.

This is his Doctrine. Here you have it. Study it and practise it.

INVERENTIAL PEACE

SAMAEL AUN WEOR

BUDDHA MAITREYA
KALKI AVATAR OF THE NEW AQUARIAN ERA

PART ONE

THE SON OF MAN

*'NOS AUTEM GLORIARI OPORTET IN CRUCE DOMINI
NOSTRI JESU-CHRISTI'*

CHAPTER 1

The Son of Man

'*B*lessed is the one who reads the words of this prophecy, and blessed are those who hear and keep what is written in it, for the time is near.' (Revelation 1:3).

Son of Man, reveal to us the things that are hidden. Each delightful symphony of the ineffable cosmos, each note, each melody that is tenderly hidden in the most pure charm of the exquisite and fragrant roses of the gardens of Nirvana is the living incarnation of your word.

The times of the end have come! '*Behold, he* (the Well-beloved One) *is coming with the clouds, and every eye will see him, every one who pierced him, and all the peoples of the earth will wail on account of him. So be it! Amen!*' (Rev. 1:7).

The Adorable One is coming! The one who has bled so much for us... The Blessed One is near! He is coming like a mother who in anguish is looking for her little children.

Listen men and gods: In the mystery of every deep wave, the Adorable One is coming. The one who makes us kings and priests for God and his Father. The evening breeze brings us orchestrations, sometimes as sweet as the lullaby of a mother, sometimes as severe as the bolt of lightning that flashes terribly amidst the catastrophic storm of the furious apocalyptic ocean.

In the ineffable and delightful depths of the Sanctuary, the Well-beloved One speaks with a voice of paradise, and says sublime things, '*I am the Alpha and the Omega, the beginning and the end, says the Lord, who is and who was and who is to come, the Almighty.'* (Rev. 1:8).

A terrible bolt of lightning flashes in the midst of the blue velvet of the starry night... It is the Son of Man! The Intimate emanates from this divine Bolt.

The choir of the saints resounds. The virgins of Nirvana sing tenderly. These virgins are deeply moved when the Bolt enters the soul of a holy man.

The ineffable Bolt enters the soul, and he is transformed into it. The Bolt is transformed into the soul and the soul into the Bolt. What is divine becomes human, and what is human becomes divine. These are the eternal nuptials of the soul and the Paschal Lamb!

From this alchemical wedding, from this mixture of love and peace, what we call the Son of Man arises. He is the shining and luminous *I Am*, our shining Dragon of Wisdom. He is the rich treasure which the Adorable One brought us.

He is the Sun-Man, Ormuzd, Osiris, Vishnu, Chur, the Lamb, the man of the time and of the river sung by Daniel.

He is the Alpha and the Omega, the First and the Last, who is and who was and who is to come. He is the Eternal Beloved, the Ancient of Days.

The Lord of all adoration wants to dwell in the depths of every soul. He is the oil of myrrh and the hill of frankincense. He is the Adorable One and the Adorer.

The expression *I Am* should be translated in this way: I Am the Being. The Well-beloved One is really the Being of our Being, who is and who was and who is to come. We have a precious tabernacle (the physical body), an anguished soul, and a spirit (the Intimate). This human triad emanated from that terribly divine Bolt that makes its tolling resound in infinite space when we come into the world.

Every man has his individual Bolt that shines with all the power of its glory in the world of the ineffable gods. That Bolt

4

of the Dawn is the Being of our Being. It is the Inner Christ of every man. It is the Sephirotic Crown of the Kabbalists, the Crown of Life. *'Be faithful until death* (says the Blessed One), *and I will give you the Crown of Life.'* (Rev. 2:10).

To the one who knows, the word gives power. No one pronounced it; no one will pronounce it, but only the one who has incarnated him.

Those who have been invited attend the wedding feast of the Paschal Lamb. Those who have incarnated him shine with glory at the angels' table. The face of the Well-beloved One is like a flash of lightning.

Christ is the Army of the Voice. Christ is the Word. In the world of the Eternal Adorable One, there is no personality, no individuality, no I. In the Lord of Supreme Adoration, we are all one. When the Well-beloved One is transformed into the soul, when the soul is transformed into the Well-beloved One, then from this ineffable — divine and human — mixture arises that which we call the Son of Man.

That Great Lord of Light — he being the Son of the Living God — becomes the Son of Man when he is transformed into the human soul. The Sun-Man is the final result of all our purifications and sorrows. The Sun-Man is both divine and human. The Son of Man is man's final result. He is the son of our sufferings. He is the solemn mystery of Transubstantiation.

Christ is the Solar Logos (Perfect Multiple Unity). Christ is the deep and unfathomable Great Eternal Breath that has emanated from the ineffable bowels of the Absolute.

Christ is our incessant eternal breath, to himself deeply unknown... Our divine Augoides.

Christ is that most pure, ineffable and terribly divine Bolt that shone like a flash of lightning on the face of Moses in the solemn mystery of Mount Nebo.

Christ is not the Monad. Christ is not the Theosophical Septenary.

Christ is not the Jivan-Atman. Christ is the Bolt that links us to the Absolute. Christ is the Central Sun.

In the East, Christ is Kwan Yin (the Melodious Voice), Avalokiteswara, Vishnu.

Among the Egyptians, Christ is Osiris, and anyone who incarnated him became Osirified.

Christ is the Atmic Thread of the Hindustanis.

The Son of Man shines with all the power of his glory in the solemn wedding-feast of the Paschal Lamb.

CHAPTER 2

The Firstborn of the Dead

J esus Christ is the faithful witness and the firstborn of the dead and the ruler of the kings of the earth, because he conquered death. *'To him who loved us and washed us from our sins by his most sacred blood'* of Adorable Martyr. (Rev. 1:5).

The Blessed One has the marvellous elixir of long life. The gift of Cupid is a grace of the Most High. The holy masters of the Guardian Wall have obtained the marvellous elixir. When a master of compassion renounces the ineffable bliss of Nirvana for the sake of this poor suffering humanity, he is entitled to ask for the gift of Cupid.

This elixir of long life is a gas that is deposited in the vital *fundus* of the human organism. Then the Initiate cries out with a loud voice, saying, *'O death! Flee before me till the end of time! You will be my slave and I will be your master!'*

The glory of the great mysteries is sublime, and the sublime images of all the Osirified Masters pass through our inner and delicate garden amidst a diffused golden and violet light.

The funeral trials of the Arcanum 13 unfold like a profound opera in the great archaic mysteries.

The austere hierophants of the great mysteries rose from the old tombs of ancient times.

In the terrifying night of the ages, the old operas of the Arcanum 13 resounded with their ineffable melodies in the underground caves of the earth.

7

To keep the body young during millions of years and never to die — this was always the greatest longing of the great masters of Alchemy.

We say: Eternal old age is better. A venerable old man, having the gift of Cupid, is always freed from the risk of falling.

Those who receive the elixir of long life die but do not die. The Lord of all compassion received the marvellous elixir of long life, and his body was embalmed for death.

On the third day, the Master of Supreme Compassion went to the Holy Sepulchre and cried out with a loud voice invoking his body. The angels of death and the holy women were with him.

When Ehecatl, Lord of Movement, entered the Holy Sepulchre, he said with a voice of paradise, 'Jesus, rise from your grave with your body!' Ehecatl, angel of cosmic movement, induced activity and movement in the body of Jesus.

As the body rose, it went into the suprasensible worlds. The physical body of Jesus plunged into the inner worlds. There the holy women, bringing aromatic drugs with them, were waiting for him in their astral bodies. They treated the body of Jesus with drugs. The body, obeying supreme orders, went into the astral body of the Master through the upper end of his sidereal head.

That is how the Adorable One rose from the dead. The body left the Holy Sepulchre and plunged into the inner worlds.

After his resurrection, Jesus appeared to the disciples of Emmaus and had supper with them. (Luke 24: 30-31). Jesus appeared also to his eleven apostles while they were gathering, and proved to them with his actions the tremendous reality of his resurrection (John 20: 19-20). The Holy Scriptures testify to the different apparitions of the Divine Master after his resurrection.

The body of the Master remained plunged in the suprasensible worlds. The body of the Divine Rabbi of Galilee went into the Jinas state. Jesus died but did not die. The Master currently lives in Shambhala in Eastern Tibet. He lives there having the

8

same body with which he rose. Other holy masters who attained the ineffable Resurrection also live in Shambhala with him.

The Great Master Zanoni attained Resurrection and kept himself young during millions of years. Unfortunately, he lost his head in the guillotine during the French Revolution. He fell for having taken a wife. He fell in love with a young Neapolitan artiste. That was his mistake.

A great Tartar Master, the body of whom is now millions of years old, told us the following: 'A true master is only the one who has swallowed soil. One, before swallowing soil, is just a fool.'

The Divine Rabbi of Galilee is the firstborn of the dead; because he, besides having risen from the dead, is the Head of the Souls.

Count of Saint Germain currently has the same physical body with which he was known during the 17th and 18th centuries in the royal courts of Europe.

After resurrection, the physical body remains in the Jinas state, that is, plunged in the suprasensible worlds. It can, however, come back into the physical world every time the Master wants to.

In these exalted conditions the Masters of Perfection live only to lead the stream of life of the countless centuries.

Condemned by themselves to live during millions of years leading the stream of centuries, those ineffable saints are the silent watchmen of the Guardian Wall. That protective wall has been raised with the blood of those saints of the Blessed One. That wall protects humanity since the dawn of creation.

The secret path is full of infinite torments. The secret pathway leads us directly to the Absolute, where the Uncreated Light shines.

Jesus Christ, the firstborn of the dead, currently lives in Shambhala. That secret country is in the Jinas state. There the Adorable Blessed One has his sacred temple.

The eastern firmament shines with all the love of the Master. The timid little flowers of the path, on which the Saint of Saints treads without harming them, tremble delightfully with the scented breeze.

The flaming fire, the pure waters of life, the earth of gentle scent, the impetuous air of Tibetan Shambhala, are all intoxicated with the glory of that Adorable Master, who is and who was and who is to come.

Mahavatar Babaji, who is keeping his body alive for several millions years now, promised to publicly teach the science that allows us to make our body of flesh and blood immortal. Here in this book this science is given.

The promise of immortal Babaji has been fulfilled.

CHAPTER 3

The Seven Churches

'*And I turned to see the voice that was speaking to me* (the 'Word' that was speaking to the Apostle), *and on turning I saw seven golden lampstands* (the seven chakras on the spinal cord, the Seven Churches), *and in the middle of the lampstands was one like a Son of Man* (a 'Word' was teaching the Apostle) *clothed with a long robe and with a golden girdle around his chest. His head and his hair were white as white wool, white as snow; his eyes were like a flame of fire, his feet were like burnished bronze, refined as in a furnace, and his voice was like the sound of many waters* (the Word, the Logos, sounds). *In his right hand he held seven stars* (in the Macrocosm, the Seven Spirits before the Throne; in the Microcosm, the seven atomic angels that govern the seven chakras or Churches of the spinal cord), *from his mouth issued a sharp two-edge sword* (the flaming sword), *and his face was like the sun shining in full strength. When I saw him, I fell at his feet as though dead. But he placed his right hand on me, saying, "Do not be afraid. I Am the first and the last".'* (Our shining Dragon of Wisdom is the first and the last). (Rev. 1:12-17).

The Well-beloved One is alive and was dead, and behold, he is alive for ever and ever. *'He has the keys of hell and death.'* (Rev. 1:18).

When we left Eden, we divorced from that Word who lives in the unknown depths of our Being. The Well-beloved One died for us, but behold, he is alive for ever and ever.

11

The Well-beloved One is Hiram murdered by three traitors. He is Jesus condemned to death by Judas, Caiaphas and Pilate. Those three traitors constitute what we call the I, the ego, the myself (Satan). Sebal, Hiram's first traitor, is Satan in the astral body of the human being. Hortelut, Hiram's second traitor, is Satan in the mind. Stokin, Hiram's third traitor, is Satan in the will-soul.

This is the I in its three fundamental levels of consciousness. This is the ruler of this world, the three-headed Black Dragon which we must decapitate and dissolve.

These are the three rebels that are within us: the demon of desire, the demon of the mind and the demon of the bad will. These are the three murderers of the Word. 'But behold, he is alive for ever and ever. Amen.'

He has the keys of our own atomic hells. *'He has the keys of hell and death.'*

We need to raise the Son of Man from the dead within ourselves.

There exist the Seven Churches in the microcosm-man and in the macrocosm.

Revelation is the book of man and of the universe. The Seven Churches of our spinal cord shine full of happiness with the sacred fire of the Holy Spirit.

The Seven Churches of our spinal cord are the doors through which we can go into the seven glorious cathedrals that are in the higher worlds.

We are filled with much fear and mystical trembling when we see the majestic cathedral in Sardis amidst flashes of lightning, peals of thunder, earthquakes, storms and heavy hail.

The laryngeal chakra is the door through which we can go into the great cathedral in Sardis.

The sublime and terribly divine church in Laodicea is all pure gold. Its dome and its walls are all carved in the most pure gold of the Spirit.

The one-thousand-petalled lotus, the shinning crown of the saints, leads us to the glorious cathedral in Laodicea — a temple that actually exists in the higher worlds.

In the Seven Churches of the inner worlds we study the rituals of life and death until the Officiant (the Word) comes.

The Seven Churches of the spinal cord are connected to the seven chakras or nerve plexuses of the sympathetic nervous system through certain very fine nerves.

The Seven Churches hang like lotus flowers from the famous Chitra Nadi. Inside the spinal canal is the Sushumna canal. Inside the Sushumna canal is the canal which we call Chitra Nadi. The Seven Churches hang beautifully and divinely from this precious spinal canal.

The spinal cord is the lampstand. On the right and left sides of the spinal cord are the two olive trees of the temple, the two olive branches that, through two golden pipes, pour oil as gold out of themselves. That golden oil is the *ens seminis*.

'These two children of oil are the ones that stand before the Lord of the whole earth.' (Zech. 4:14). These are the Two Witnesses (Ida and Pingala). This is the pair of sympathetic nerves coiling like two serpents around the spinal cord. The oil of pure gold ascends to the chalice (brain) along them.

When the metal serpent awakens, it then goes into the *canalis centralis* of the spinal cord and ascends very slowly and with much difficulty along that spinal canal called Brahma Nadi in India.

The Seven Churches shine with the consuming fire of the Holy Spirit. As the sacred fire ascends, the Seven Churches become opened and turn upwards. As the Seven Churches open, then the chakras, or sympathetic plexuses, awaken.

The lampstand has seven lamps, which are the Seven Churches, and seven canals for the lamps that are above it. These seven canals correspond to the seven degrees of power of the fire.

13

All these chakras, discs, magnetic wheels, are the senses of the astral body.

Our soul is wrapped in the astral body. The astral body has its ultrasensible anatomy, physiology and pathology.

The senses of the astral body and the endocrine glands are in close relationship. Wherever there is a nerve plexus, there is also a chakra of the astral body.

Inside our astral body is our mind, our will, our consciousness, our spirit, etc.

When the Seven Churches awaken, our astral body is filled with glory and beauty.

That is how we become totally transfigured and glorified.

CHAPTER 4

The Metal Serpent

Between the woman and the serpent there is enmity ever since we left Eden. The serpent deceived Eve and from that moment the conflict started. Jehovah said to the serpent: *'Because you have done this, cursed are you among all cattle and among all wild animals; on your belly you will go, and dust you will eat all the days of your life. And I will put enmity between you and the woman, and between your seed and her seed; it will bruise your head, and you will bruise its heel.'* (Genesis 3:14-15).

The world was filled with tears ever since the serpent was cursed. The woman bruises the serpent's head, and the serpent takes revenge on the woman by bruising her heel. Then we are born crying and we die crying.

In the desert Moses raised the Metal Serpent on the rod. That serpent was turned into the very rod itself. The fight is terrible: *Brain against sex, sex against brain and heart against heart.* We have to tame and raise the Metal Serpent on the rod as Moses did in the desert.

We have to go down to the Ninth Sphere (sex), to work with the fire and the water, origin of worlds, beasts, men and gods. Every genuine white initiation begins there. In the union of the phallus and the womb lies the key to all power. Lift your cup well and take care not to spill even a single drop of the sacred wine. Kill desire. Kill even the very shadow of desire. We have to celebrate the Wedding of Cana and to transmute the water into wine. When a man is chaste, he can raise the Igneous Serpent of

15

our Magical Powers along the central canal of his spinal cord. The Pentecostal Fire has the power to open the Seven Churches. When the solar atoms make contact with the lunar atoms in the coccygeal bone near the triveni, then the sacred fire of Pentecost comes to us. The Igneous Serpent rises from the sacred depths of the Ark. That Ark of the Testament symbolizes the sexual organs.

In the Holy of Holies of the Temple of Solomon the Ark shone like a terribly divine flash of lightning. On the right and left sides of the Ark of Science were two Cherubim that touched each other with their wings. Those two most sacred Cherubim were in the attitude of a man and of a woman during sexual intercourse.

Within the Ark were the rod of Aaron (symbol of the phallus), the cup or gomor containing the manna of the desert (symbol of the womb) and the Tables of the Law, without which the development of the terrible Metal Serpent is impossible.

That divine serpent is called Kundalini. Devi Kundalini awakens only with the ineffable charms of love. The important thing is not to waste the sacred wine. Only willpower can save us in the wine-chamber. Kundalini goes up slowly along the spinal canal. The Seven Churches are on the spinal canal. Kundalini opens the Seven Churches.

The beautiful, immaculate and divine white light which angels radiate comes from the lampstand of their spinal cords.

The spinal cord is the sacred lampstand of the Temple.

The lampstand of solid gold that was in the Temple of Solomon had seven arms. This lampstand represents the spinal cord with its Seven Churches.

On the right and left sides of the lampstand are the two olive trees of the Temple, *the two children of oil.*

When we work with the A.Z.F. Arcanum, then the water and the fire of the Ninth Sphere go up along these two sympathetic canals (Ida and Pingala) to the chalice (brain).

16

The holy martyr Miguel de Molinos said, *'The subtlest arrow which nature shoots at us is to induce us to do what is unlawful* (fornication) *on the pretext of being something necessary and beneficial. Oh! How many souls have allowed themselves to be led astray and even have lost the spirit through this gilded deception! They will never taste the silent Manna. QUOD NEMO NOCET NISI QUI ACCIPIT.*

'If you do not perfectly conquer yourself (the animal I) *until you die in yourself; because he who does not seek to die to his passions is not ready to receive the gift of understanding, without the infusion of which it is impossible that he can go into introversion and be transformed into the Spirit. That is why those who are outside live without Him.*

'Resign and deny yourself in everything. For although real self-denial is sour in the beginning; it is easy in the middle, and it is very mild in the end. You will know that you are very far away from perfection if you do not find God in all things. You will know that pure, perfect and essential love lies in the Cross, in one's voluntary denial and resignation, in one's perfect humility, poverty of spirit and self-contempt.

'In times of rigorous temptation, forsakenness and desolation, it matters that you go into yourself and be in the innermost part of your centre, so that you may only look at and contemplate God, who has his throne and stillness in the depths of your soul. You will experience that the impatience and bitterness of the heart have their origins in the depths of the empty and unmortified sensible love. True love and its effects can be known when the soul profoundly humbles itself and it truly wants to be mortified and despised.'

If you want to light your seven-armed lampstand, remember that this is the path of the razor's edge. This path is full of dangers inside and outside.

CHAPTER 5

Inner Meditation

In the school of Sufism we find a description of the seven degrees of ecstasy through which the mystic reaches the perfect state of the soul.

Sufism is the school of ecstasy. The 'station of the level with the secret' is revealed there, because it is the inner state of life in God.

In the path of inner peace we must do the will of the Father, on earth as it is in heaven. This conformity with the 'light yoke' leads us to the light along the narrow and difficult road.

All those who work in the Magistery of Fire must learn to mediate on the Seven Churches.

The mystic must concentrate deeply on the Immolated Lamb. The mystic must pray, entreating the Adorable One to awaken the chakra, disc, wheel or longed-for faculty.

Once the supplication has been made, the mystic must seek his refuge in Nothing. The mind must become quiet and still.

When the mind is silent, when the mind is still, then enlightenment, ecstasy, comes.

Sleep combined with meditation produces ecstasy.

God seeks Nothing to fill it.

Ecstasy has seven degrees of power: The first degree is the fire that instructs us and teaches us.

The second is the Gnostic Unction. This is a gentle solar liquor which, when it diffuses through the entire soul, teaches it, strengthens it and prepares it to incarnate truth.

The third is the mystical exaltation of the humble and sincere disciple.

The fourth is Enlightenment.

The fifth is the inner bliss of the divine sweetness emanated from the precious fountain of the Holy Spirit.

This delight is for those who have continuous consciousness.

The sixth is the decapitation of the I.

The seventh is Venusta Initiation, the incarnation of the Son of Man within ourselves.

There are other degrees of contemplation and ecstasy, such as: raptures, liquefaction, deliquium, jubilation, osculum, embrace, transformation, etc.

When our mind plunges into Nothing, the Lamb enters the soul to have supper with it. That Nothing is the medium by which the Well-beloved One can act in your soul, awakening centres and performing wonders. The divine groom comes through that Nothing to wed his soul in the nuptial chamber of Paradise.

Thus, through this way, we return to the innocence of Paradise. The soul, plunged into that Nothing, will go successfully through the spiritual ordeals and inner torments. God seeks Nothing to fill it.

Inner meditation produces changes in our inner bodies. Then the awakening of consciousness comes. All the human beings are in the suprasensible worlds with their consciousness asleep. Meditation causes the solemn awakening of consciousness.

That awakening is like a flash of lightning in the night. The awakening of consciousness comes during the normal sleep of our physical body. When the body is asleep we move in our inner vehicles.

When the body is asleep, the soul travels through the higher worlds. With the awakening of consciousness we stop dreaming. Then we are in the inner worlds in a state of intensified watchfulness. That is what is called *continuous consciousness*.

Those who have awakened consciousness are continuously awake in the higher worlds.

In the suprasensible worlds we feel the mystical beatitude of the ineffable light.

There the past and the future merge into the eternal now.

There is no greater pleasure than that of feeling one's soul freed.

Then we savour the divine nectar of Eternalness and full of joy we go in through the doors of the Temples amidst the ineffable melodies of the Great Mysteries.

CHAPTER 6

The Church of Ephesus

The Church of Ephesus is exactly situated between the sexual organs and the anus. This is the coccygeal church. The sacred serpent, shut in its silent stillness, is asleep in this church, awaiting the supreme instant of its awakening. The marvellous serpent awakens amidst the miraculous charms of love. Mozart's Magic Flute reminds us of the profound mysteries of the sacred serpent.

The Church of Ephesus is a mystical lotus flower. This flower has four petals, and anyone who meditates deeply on the Church of Ephesus goes into the underground regions of the earth. Then the gnomes, or pygmies, teach us their mysteries. The tattwa Prithvi shines with glory in the Church of Ephesus.

The lingam-yoni mysteries are hidden in the Church of Ephesus.

'To the angel of the church in Ephesus write (the Word speaks to the atomic angel of the Church of Ephesus): *"These are the words* (the virtues needed to open the Church of Ephesus) *of the one who holds the seven stars in his right hand* (The Son of Man), *who walks among the seven golden lampstands* (the seven-armed lampstands). *I know your works, your toil and your patient endurance* (patient endurance is the condition needed to open this church), *and how you cannot tolerate evil men but have tested those who call themselves apostles but are not, and have found them to be false* (because they are fornicators). *I know you are enduring patiently and bearing up for the sake of*

my name, (by suffering and by patient endurance we open the church of Ephesus) *and you have not grown weary. But I have this against you, that you have forsaken your first love* (the first love is the Eternal Beloved, the Inner God, the Ineffable One. When the soul leaves the Well-beloved One, it then suffers terribly). *Remember then from what you have fallen, repent and do the works you did at first* (creating without fornicating). *If not, I will come to you and remove your lampstand from its place, unless you repent.* (When man spills the sacred wine of the temple, he commits a sacrilege. Then the serpent of fire goes down one or more vertebras according to the magnitude of the offence. The lampstand is therefore removed from its place, and the pain caused by remorse will afflict your heart). *Yet this you have, you hate the works of the Nicolaitans, which I also hate."'* (Rev. 2:1-6).

When the priest spills the sacred wine of the altar, the blessed Goddess Mother of the world covers her face with her veil and weeps bitterly. Then the Well-Beloved One crucifies himself on his cross and the whole of nature shudders full of terror.

The sacred wine is the semen of Benjamin. That semen, contained in the chalice of Benjamin, Jacob's beloved son, is a mixture of wine and water.

When the priest spills the wine of the temple, the enchanted serpent goes down to man's atomic hells and becomes the tail of Satan.

In ancient times there were giants on the earth who committed that sacrilege.

The cities of Carthage, Tyre and Sidon were also razed to the ground because of that crime. The Canaanites too committed that sacrilege.

The Mysteries of Vulcan were betrayed, and man sank into the abyss.

'Those are the works of the Nicolaitans which I also hate.' (Rev. 2:6).

CHAPTER 7

The Church of Smyrna

The Church of Smyrna is the prostatic chakra. Apas is the tattwa of this chakra. *'You will be all gods if you go out of Egypt and cross the Red Sea.'*

There sings the divine man. There sings the ineffable woman. There sing both, man and woman. Both sing the sublime opera of the ages. That opera of light begins in Eden and ends in Eden. The sublime man's voice is heroic; it is awesome like a flashing bolt of lightning, like an all-powerful clap of thunder. Her voice is as sweet and melodious as Mozart's Magic Flute, or as the miraculous voice of a mermaid of the vast ocean. This moving duo, this love *connubium* of the Word makes the waters of life fertile.

When the serpent of fire breathes on the waters of Eden, the Church of Smyrna opens amidst the august thundering of thought.

Let us kneel down to contemplate the miraculous six-petalled lotus, the lotus of the Nile, the prostatic chakra on which the nereids of the immense ocean settle.

Pray and meditate on the prostatic chakra. When the Well-Beloved One awakens this chakra, we become elemental kings of waters.

This chakra gives us conscious consciousness about the nature of all beings inhabiting the inner worlds.

Those who drink of the pure waters of life will never be thirsty again. These most pure waters of Eden are the divine mirror of love.

The swan of inviolable whiteness settles on the lotus flower. The swan of love awakens amidst nature's moving love-whispers.

'And to the (atomic) *angel of the church in Smyrna write: "These are the words of the first and the last, who died and came to life again* (in anyone receiving Venusta Initiation). *I know your tribulation and your poverty* (tribulation and poverty are essential conditions to open the Church of Smyrna); *but you are rich* (spiritually). *I know the slander of those who say they are Jews and are not, but are a synagogue of Satan. Do not fear what you are about to suffer. Behold, the devil is about to throw some of you into prison* (the prison of pain), *so that you may be tested, and you will have tribulation for ten days* (that is, you will have tribulation as long as you are subjected to the wheel of reincarnation and Karma). *Be faithful until death, and I will give you the crown of life.'* (Rev. 2:8-10).

Those who receive the Crown of Life are freed from the wheel of reincarnation and Karma.

The Crown of Life is triune. It has three aspects: First, the Ancient of Days; second, the adorable Son, and third, the most wise Holy Spirit.

The Crown of Life is the Sun-Man, the Sun-King who was so celebrated by Emperor Julian. The Crown of Life is our Endless Eternal Breath, to itself deeply unknown. It is every man's individual Bolt of Lightning, the Christ. The Crown of Life is Kether, Chokmah and Binah (Father, Son and Holy Spirit).

Those who are faithful until death receive the Crown of Life.

At the wedding feast of the Lamb the ineffable faces of all those saints who have incarnated him shine like suns of love. The immaculate white table cloth is stained with real blood of the Immolated Lamb.

'*"He who has an ear, let him hear what the Spirit says to the churches. He who conquers will not be hurt by the second death."*' (Rev. 2:11).

He who does not conquer will divorce from the Well-Beloved One and will sink into the abyss. Those who enter the abyss will go through the second death. The demons of the abyss disintegrate slowly through many eternities. Those souls are lost. He who conquers will not be hurt by the second death.

'*Be faithful until death, and I will give you the crown of life.*' (Rev. 2:10).

To the one who knows, the word gives power. No one pronounced it; no one will pronounce it, but only the one who has incarnated him.

When we receive the Crown of Life, the Word becomes flesh in every one of us.

Every saint who attains Venusta Initiation receives the Crown of Life.

Our most beloved Saviour Jesus Christ attained Venusta Initiation in the Jordan.

'*And the Word became flesh and dwelt among us, and we have seen his glory, glory as of the only son of the Father, full of grace and truth.*' (John 1:14).

'*The light came into the darkness, but the darkness did not know it.*' (John 3:19).

He is the Saviour, because he brought us the Crown of Life and gave his blood for us.

We need to attain the supreme annihilation of the I, so that we can receive the Crown of Life.

We need to raise the Lamb within ourselves. We need Easter Resurrection.

CHAPTER 8

The Church of Pergamum

Eden is the blessed womb of the Goddess Mother of the world. We left Eden through the door of sex, and only through that door can we go back into Eden. In the Garden of Eden there are two very old trees: the tree of the knowledge of good and evil and the tree of life.

'When the woman saw that the tree was good for food, and that it was a delight to the eyes, and that the tree was to be desired to make one wise, she took of its fruit and ate, and she also gave some to her husband, and he ate. Then the eyes of both were opened, and they knew that they were naked, and they sewed fig leaves together and made aprons for themselves.' (Genesis 3:6-7).

Eighteen million years have passed and we are still naked. If we want to return to Eden, we must dress as kings and priests of nature after the Order of Melchizedek, King of Fire.

The Church of Pergamum is the church of fire. This chakra is a fair lotus flower with ten very beautiful petals that are saturated with happiness. This chakra is situated in the region of the navel and controls the liver, stomach, etc. The colour of this chakra is like the colour of the clouds laden with lightning and living fire. In this chakra is a triangular space. The region of fire, the region of the Agni Tattwa, is in that ineffable space.

By meditating on this chakra we will be able to walk through fire without getting burnt. Whoever develops this chakra will not be afraid of fire, and will be able to remain surrounded by fire for hours on end without being harmed.

'*And the three men, Shadrach, Meshack and Abednego, fell down, bound, into the furnace of blazing fire. Then king Nebuchadnezzar was astonished and rose up quickly. He said to his counsellors, "Was it not three men that we threw bound into the fire?" They answered the king, "True, O king." He replied, "But I see four men unbound, walking in the middle of the fire, and they are not hurt; and the fourth has the appearance of a son of the gods." Nebuchadnezzar then approached the door of the furnace of blazing fire and said, "Shadrach, Meshach and Abednego, servants of the Most High God, come out! Come here!" So Shadrach, Meshach and Abednego came out from the fire. And the satraps, the prefects, the governors and the king's counsellors gathered together and saw that the fire had not had any power over the bodies of those men; the hair of their heads was not singed, their tunics were not harmed, and not even the smell of fire came from them.*' (Daniel 3:23-27).

When we meditate on this chakra, we enter Eden. There we find the human beings still naked. Only we the Brothers of the Temple are dressed in the clothes of fire. By developing this chakra we become Kings of Fire. When the Sacred Serpent ascends and reaches the region of the navel, the Church of Pergamum opens. By internally meditating on this beautiful lotus in the abdomen we are given the power to govern fire.

Fan the flame of the spirit with the divine nectar of love.

Fire burns up the dross of evil. Drive the demons of desire out of the sanctuary of your soul.

Your soul must be as pure as the dewdrop, which when vibrating with love, plunges delightfully into the fragrant petals of roses. Protect your soul against the snares of the I. Kill not only desire, but even the very shadows of the tree of desire.

Remember that the christonic semen is the *Prima Materia* (First Matter) of the Great Work. Cleanse your soul from every desire. Be chaste. If you are sure of having annihilated every desire, analyse yourself in depth; search thoroughly very deep within your soul. It may happen that the I is betraying you in other levels of consciousness.

Subjugate your senses. Control your mind. Kill every desire to live. Desire nothing.

'*And to the* (atomic) *Angel of the church in Pergamum write: "These are the words of the one who has the sharp two-edged sword* (the Son of Man): *I know where you dwell, where Satan's throne is* (Satan's throne is in the region of the navel. Nevertheless, the atomic angel of Pergamum is faithful). *You hold fast my name, and you did not deny my faith even in the days of Antipas, my faithful witness, who was killed among you, where Satan dwells.'* (Rev. 2:12-13). Antipas was a man who really existed. That man was a holy martyr who was murdered when he was preaching the word of the Lord. That place where Antipas was murdered was really a dwelling place of Satan. It was a synagogue of Satan. This was a historic event.

In the chakra of the navel is a dark nuclear atom. The I is closely related to that atom. That is Satan's throne.

'*"But I have a few things against you: You have some there who hold the teaching of Balaam, who taught Balak to put a stumbling block before the sons of Israel, so that they would eat food sacrificed to idols and practise fornication.* (All these vulgar passions belong to Satan. Satan's throne is in the region of the navel. Gluttony, drunkenness,etc., are in the area of the stomach). *So you also have some who hold the teaching of the Nicolaitans, which I hate.'* (Rev. 2:14-15).

Only sanctity and absolute chastity can turn us into angels. The Nicolaitans spill the sacred wine of the temple. They waste the oil of the lamp and are left in darkness. The Nicolaitans spill the *Prima Materia* of the Great Work in practices of sexual alchemy. That is black tantrism.

'*"Repent then. If not, I will come to you soon and make war against them with the sword of my mouth.'* (Rev. 2:16). This is happening now. We must know that since the year 1950 a

'Word' is fighting against them with the flaming sword. The Nicolaitans are sinking into the abyss. The Nicolaitans became terribly wicked demons.

"He who has an ear, let him hear what the Spirit says to the churches. To him who conquers I will give some of the hidden manna (the manna of christic wisdom), *and I will give him a white stone* (the philosopher's stone, sex), *with a new name written on the stone, which no one knows except the one who receives it."* (Rev. 2:17).

That new name is the name of our Inner God, the name of the Son of Man.

The virtues needed to open the Church of Pergamum are: chastity, loyalty, faith and obedience to the Father.

An Initiate cannot be either gluttonous or a drunkard or a fornicator. The Nicolaitans, by fornicating, develop dark magical powers.

Initiates must be temperate, faithful, chaste, humble and obedient.

CHAPTER 9

The Church of Thyatira

When the Serpentine Fire reaches the region of the heart, the Church of Thyatira opens. Prayer and inner meditation develop and unfold the chakra of the tranquil heart. In the heart are seven sacred centres which correspond to the seven degrees of power of the fire. The heart is the sanctuary of love.

Beware of sensual love. Do not mix selfish love with sacred ecstasy. Love is as pure as the morning star. Love is universal. Love is impersonal, ineffable, unselfish.

Be charitable. When we criticize other people's religion, we sin against Christian charity. Cultivate respect and veneration. Respect other people's beliefs. Respect your neighbour's religion. Do not try to force others to think as you think. Do not criticize. Remember that every head is a world. Do not sin against the charity of the Christ any more.

Humanity is divided and subdivided into groups. Every group needs its special system of teaching. Every group needs its school, its religion, its sect.

Those are the Commandments of the Blessed One.

When we criticize others, we violate the law of the tranquil heart.

If you are able to give even the last drop of your blood for the sake of this poor suffering humanity, you are then one of ours.

Whoever wants to reach the altar of initiation must become a 'lamb' immolated on the altar of supreme sacrifice.

It is necessary to love those who hate us, to kiss the adorable hand of the one who flogs us, to clean the sandals of the one who humiliates us.

If a poor beggar invites you to his table, eat with him, because that poor beggar is our brother. If a leper breaks a loaf of bread and offers you a piece of it, take it and eat it, because that poor leper is your brother; do not despise him.

Be always the last one. Do not aspire to be the first. Sit down in the lowest places. Never sit down in the best place. Remember that you are just a poor sinner. Do not think that you are perfect because only your Father who is in secret is perfect. Your inner God is full of glory, but you are just a poor worm that crawls through the mud. You are not perfect.

Bear no resentment against any fellow human being. Remember that they are not perfect either. Do not be spiteful or vindictive. Love, forgive, kiss with love the hand of the tormentor who flogs you. It is necessary that your I should be annihilated so that that Great Lord of Light can come into your soul.

Dress in light, my brother. Hear the ten mystical sounds of the tranquil heart. The first sound is like the voice of the Son of Man fertilizing the waters of Genesis so that life can spring. The second is the Chin-Bhini sound. The third is the supreme sound of the great cosmic bell, which emanates from the inner ray of every man. The fourth is the inner din of the earth, whose solemn vibrations are repeated in the body of every man. The fifth is like the delightful sound of the lute. The sixth is the cymbal of the ineffable gods, resounding in the calyx of every blessed flower. The seventh sound is that of the enchanted flute, whose virginal melodies take us to the supreme bliss of the gardens of Nirvana. The eighth sound is that of the bass drum. The ninth is the sound of the exotic variation of a double drum. The tenth is the sound of the seven thunderclaps repeating their voices.

When we, being crucified on the cross of Golgotha, arrive at the ninth hour, we cry out in a loud voice saying, 'Father, into your hands I commend my spirit.' (Luke 23:46) The supreme instant of the ninth hour comes amidst terrible flashes of lightning, and words and voices and thunder (the seven thunderclaps repeat the voices of the Eternal).

Only those who have gone through the supreme death of the I, of the myself, of the ego, can pronounce the Seventh Word.

The fight with Satan was a terrible fight. A woman always shuts the initiates' tomb with a big stone (the philosopher's blessed stone).

The supreme spear of pain pierces the heart of the great initiates, and blood and water come up from their wounds.

The *Prima Materia* of the Great Work is the sacred wine.

By meditating internally on the lotus of the heart you will hear the ten mystical sounds. By meditating on the lotus of the heart we will control the Vayu Tattva, and we will be given power over winds and hurricanes. The lotus of the heart has fifteen petals shining with the fire of the Holy Spirit.

In the chakra of the heart is a hexagonal space of the ineffable colour of jet. The ten mystical sounds of the Church of Thyatira resound there like a symphony of Beethoven. The great rhythms of the Mahavan and of the Chotavan keep the universe steady in its course. The rhythms of fire are the foundation of the exquisite harmonies of the cosmic diapason. If you visit Nirvana during an ecstasy you must fulfil the sacred duty of singing there in accordance with the rhythms of fire. Thus you help us with your speech. The universe is sustained by the Word.

If you want to learn to travel consciously in the inner worlds, you must develop the chakra of the heart.

If you want to reach the Christ, kill desire. Be like lemon. If you want to learn how to put your body in the Jinas state, you must develop the chakra of the heart. Through the system of inner meditation we can develop the chakra of the tranquil heart.

'And to the (atomic) *angel of the church in Thyatira write: "These are the words of the Son of God, who has eyes like a flame of fire, and whose feet are like burnished bronze. I know your works, your love, faith, service and patient endurance, and that your latter works exceed the first.'* (Rev. 2:18-19). Love (charity), service, faith and patient endurance. These are the virtues needed to open the Church of Thyatira.

'"But I have this against you, that you tolerate that woman Jezebel, who calls herself a prophetess and is teaching and beguiling my servants to practise fornication and to eat food sacrificed to idols.' (Rev. 2:20).

Jezebel symbolizes the harlot dressed in purple and scarlet. She is the intellectual mind that teaches us how to fornicate and how to eat things sacrificed to idols. Jezebel is politics, journalism, diplomacy, materialistic science, intellectualism of all kinds, etc. In ancient times Jezebel taught men how to eat food sacrificed to idols in the temples of black magic. Jezebel means intellectualism, banqueting, drunkenness, orgies, gluttony, fornication, adultery, materialistic science, etc. The symbols of Jezebel are the turkey and the pig.

'"I gave her time to repent, but she refuses to repent of her fornication. Behold, I will throw her on a bed, and I will throw those who commit adultery with her into great tribulation, unless they repent of her doings.' (Rev. 2:21-22). Jezebel is the satanic mind that has refused to repent of her evil works. The times of the end have already come and Jezebel and all those who commit adultery with her will be thrown into beds of pain. The dwellers of the earth, the magnates of gold and silver, the vultures of war and the intellectuals who hate the Eternal, all commit adultery with Jezebel.

'"And I will strike her children dead (the children of Jezebel are the dwellers of the earth, the intellectuals and the merchants of fine linen and of gold and of silver, and of silk and of scarlet, and of all kinds of valuable wood, and of copper and of iron and of marble). *And all the churches will know that I am the one who searches kidneys and hearts, and I will give to each of you according to your works.'* (Rev. 2:23).

36

When the renal chakras shine with immaculate whiteness like a lotus flower, it is because we have attained supreme chastity.

When the renal chakras are stained with a colour of blood and passion. Woe to us, because we are fornicators, and the Word throws us into the abyss with his sword. Woe to the dwellers of the earth!

The Word searches the kidneys and hearts and gives to each of us according to our works.

Whoever wants to open the Church of Thyatira must have a child's mind. Those who commit adultery with Jezebel (who calls herself a prophetess) cannot know the wisdom of the tranquil heart.

The secret path of the heart is wisdom and love. The wisdom of the seal of the heart is for children, that is, for those who do not commit adultery with Jezebel (who calls herself a prophetess). If you want to open the Church of Thyatira, you must reconquer your lost childhood. Jezebel is Satan. Jezebel is the I, the myself, the ego that is within us.

'*"But to the rest of you in Thyatira, who do not hold this teaching, who have not learned what some call the deep things of Satan, to you I say, I do not lay on you any other burden; only hold fast what you have until I come. To him who conquers and who keeps my works until the end, I will give power over the nations, and he will rule them with an iron rod, as when clay pots are broken in pieces, just as I also received authority from my Father. And I will give him the morning star. He who has an ear, let him hear what the Spirit says to the churches."*' (Rev. 2: 24-29).

When we decapitate and dissolve the I, the myself, we then receive Venusta Initiation. Anyone who receives Venusta Initiation incarnates his or her star. It is urgent to know that the star crucified on the cross is the Christ of the Abraxas.

The star is the Son of Man, truth. No one can seek truth. Truth cannot be known by the I. No one can seek truth. No one can seek what they do not know. Jezebel (who calls herself a prophetess) cannot know truth. Truth cannot be studied, read or recognized by the mind. Truth is absolutely different to everything that can be read, studied or recognized by the mind. Truth comes to us when we have decapitated and dissolved the I.

People's different truths are just projections of the mind. The times of the end have already come, and all who commit adultery with Jezebel (who calls herself a prophetess) will be broken in pieces like clay pots.

When a devotee enters the chamber of the pure spirit, he or she feels a delightful terror. That sacred chamber is lit by an immaculate and divine light which gives life and casts no shadow on anyone's way. All those who have reached the heights of contemplation and enlightenment will see the living picture of the event of Golgotha in this chamber of the pure spirit. No genius of the earth could have been able to paint so much beauty. That picture has life of its own. The stigmas of the Adorable One bleed, and his blood stains the soil of Golgotha red. His most beloved temples, pierced by the cruel thorns of the crown of torment, bleed painfully, and blood and water flow from his side, wounded by the spear of Longinus. That picture has life in abundance. The sun sets into its bed of purple. At the foot of the cross of Calvary are the skulls of those who were put to death and the shadow of death. Do not be afraid, faithful devotee. Look, the shadow of death rises. Do not be afraid. Conquer it.

Remember that the Lord conquered death. *'Flee from before me until the end of the ages. You will be my slave, and I will be your Master.'*

It fled, but look what is in the middle of the Sanctuary: He is the administrator. Look at him! He is a gigantic spectre dressed as the princes dressed in the Middle Ages.

He is the ruler of this world, haughty and wicked. He is your own I.

Decapitate him with your flaming sword, and then dissolve him through rigorous purifications.

In that way you will reach Venusta Initiation.

Then you will incarnate Truth.

The Word will become flesh in you.

You will incarnate the Son of Man, and you will receive the Morning Star.

CHAPTER 10

The Church of Sardis

When the serpentine fire, ascending victoriously, reaches the region of the thyroid gland, the Church of Sardis opens.

The laryngeal chakra has sixteen beautiful petals that shine full of glory with the sacred Fire of Pentecost.

This beautiful chakra looks like a mysterious full moon, shining like an ineffable poem amidst the moving melodies of the infinite ether. By meditating deeply on this chakra, its hidden and terrible powers will awaken. With the development of the laryngeal chakra we can keep our body alive even during the great cosmic nights, without the Pralaya being able to disintegrate it. With the development of the laryngeal chakra we obtain conceptual syntheticism. The great Masters of Nirvana do not reason.

Conceptual syntheticism and intuition will replace the process of reasoning. Desire and reasoning belong to the I. Satan is really the reasoner. With the development of the laryngeal chakra we understand the esoterism of holy books. The Akasha Tattwa is the tattwa of the laryngeal chakra. With the development of the laryngeal chakra we will know the past, the present and the future of everything existing in the universe. With the development of the laryngeal chakra our sacred ear will awaken, and we will be able to hear the words of Paradise and the ineffable symphonies of the temples. With the development of the laryngeal chakra we receive the power of understanding. Understanding and intuition will replace reason.

An understanding mind does not judge or translate. The I judges and translates everything that it sees into the language of its prejudices, memories, errors and evil deeds.

'Do not judge, so that you may not be judged. For with the judgement you make you will be judged, and the measure you give will be the measure you get.' (Matthew 7:1-2). Be all the time in a state of perception-alertness. See, hear and understand. Do not judge, so that you may not be judged. Understand everything. Do not turn Satan into a translator of everything you see and hear.

Reconquer the innocence of Eden. You, who meditate on the Church of Sardis, listen to the ineffable words of Nirvana. Have you ever attended the Nirvanis' banquet?

Look! What divine beings! These holy Masters are dressed in diamond robes, the robes of Dharmasayas. On the banquet table are three vessels containing three most pure balms. The first is the red balm of fire. The second is the green balm of the pure water that gives eternal life. The third is the immaculate and pure white balm of the spirit.

Drink from those three vessels, and you will never be thirsty again.

Ah!... When your words are pure and beautiful like the voices of Paradise. Ah! When your every sentence is love, beauty, harmony... Then your creative larynx will be like the divine and enchanting notes of a piano of Nirvana, like the melody of a temple, like the speech of those holy Masters who attend the banquet of the Immolated Lamb.

Never speak vain words. Never say immodest words.

The throat is a womb where speech is gestated. The gods create with the power of speech. Kundalini is creative with the power of speech. Kundalini is creative in the larynx. The sexual organ of the gods is the creative larynx.

'In the beginning was the Word, and the Word was with God, and the Word was God. He was in the beginning with God. All

things were made through him, and without him was not any-thing made that was made.' (John 1:1-3). The Army of the Voice is the Christ.

When life dawned, the gods taught us the divine laws by singing in their golden language.

When the heart of the solar system started to beat after the deep night, the Army of the Voice fertilized the chaos so that life could spring.

The Seven Sublime Lords sang the rhythms of fire. The gods and their Isises officiated in every one of the seven temples. Every one of the Seven and their Isises sang the rituals of fire. In every one of the Seven Churches were a priest, an Isis and a choir of angels (man, woman, choir).

The sexual *connubium* of creative speech fertilized the wa-ters of the chaos so that life could spring. That is how the uni-verse came into being. The sexual fire of the Word fertilized the waters of Genesis.

In the beginning the universe was subtle, pure and ineffable. After successive condensations, the universe acquired its pres-ent dense, coarse, material state.

'And to the (atomic) *angel of the church in Sardis write: "These are the words of the one who has the seven spirits of God and the seven stars. I know your works; you have a name* (of your Inner God) *of being alive, but you are dead* (because you have not incarnated him). *Awake, and strengthen what remains and is about to die* (confirm the death of your I), *for I have not found your works perfect in the sight of my God.'* (Rev. 3:1-2).

Remember that all the works of the I are bad. Resolve to die. Take the food of the I from it, and it will disintegrate. Faults are the food of the I. Do not justify your faults. Do not condemn them. Understand them. When we become consciously con-scious of our own faults, they disintegrate. The I, without food, dies. First, Satan has to be decapitated, and then dissolved. You know it.

'"Remember then what you received and heard; keep that, and repent. If you do not wake up, I will come like a thief, and you will not know at what hour I will come to you.' (Rev. 3:3). Remember that the times of the end have already come. We are in them. The great cataclysm of fire will come any minute now. You know it. The Lord will come like a thief in the night when least expected.

'"Yet you have still a few people in Sardis who have not soiled their garments, and they will walk with me, dressed in white, for they are worthy. He who conquers will be clothed in white garments, and I will not blot his name out of the book of life; I will confess his name before my Father and before his angels (whoever incarnates him is a conqueror). *He who has an ear, let him hear what the Spirit says to the churches."'* (Rev 3:4-6). Remember that the sacred wine is the *ens seminis*. You know it.

All the power of the Word is contained in the *ens seminis*. The insertion of the vertical *phallus* into the horizontal *cteis* forms the *stauros* of the Gnostics. The cteis is the house of the phallus. Creation is the house of the Word. In the cteis and phallus, both well united, lies the secret key for awakening the Fire. The important thing is to avoid orgasm in order to prevent the *Prima Materia* of the Great Work from going out of its container. Our device is *Thelema* (will). In the *ens seminis* is contained all the *ens virtutis* of the sacred fire. Nevertheless, as some medical practitioners maintain that this scientific operation can harm us (*loedere*) in several ways; we say that this is not so, since the *ens seminis* is completely transmuted into light and fire. It happens that in our creative organs there is a slow boiling (*digerere*), which reduces the *ens seminis* to its primordial energy principles. The solar and lunar atoms of the seminal system ascend to the brain along its two sympathetic canals. These two canals are two fine cords that ascend from the testes to the brain. These canals are called Ida and Pingala in the East. These are the two witnesses. Light the Fire so that you can incarnate

44

the Word. Without the Fire you cannot speak the Golden Language of the first instant.

When the solar and lunar atoms make contact in the coccyx, then the Igneous Serpent of our Magical Powers awakens, and we become burning flames.

The insertion of the vertical phallus into the formal cteis is the key of Fire. However, be careful not to spill the sacred wine of the temple. Raise your cup. Do not spill the wine of the altar. In the *ens seminis* are the atoms of those languages which we spoke in our past lives. When those atomic substances of speech ascend to the creative larynx, then we speak again those languages. Only the Holy Spirit can give us the gift of tongues.

In the *ens seminis* are also transformative atoms of very high voltage. Those atoms transform us completely.

In the *ens seminis* are the atoms of the cosmic grammar. The most pure *orthos* of the divine language flows like a golden river beneath the thick forest of the sun.

When the Word becomes flesh in us, we have attained perfect beatitude. He who conquers will be clothed in white garments because he is a Master of the Day, a Master of the Mahamanvantara. *'His name will be written in the book of life, and I will confess his name before my Father and before the angels.'*

It is necessary to be born again in order to enter the Kingdom of Heaven.

The Word is always born of Immaculate Conceptions. The Word is always a child of the most pure virgins. The mother of the Word is always a woman. Jesus, bleeding and full of pain, crucified on his cross, said to his mother the following words: *'Woman, here is your son.'* (John 19:26). Referring to John who was beside Mary. *'Then he said to the disciple, "Here is your mother." And from that hour the disciple* (John) *took her into his own home.'* (John 19:27).

'John' is broken down into the five vowels, in this way: I.E.O.U.A.N.

Mantrams are formed with these five vowels. John is the Great Word.

'Truly, truly, I say to you, unless a person is born of water (semen) *and of the spirit* (fire), *he cannot enter the Kingdom of God.'* (John 3:5) All the first twenty-one verses of chapter three of Saint John contain the Great Arcanum.

The A.Z.F. Arcanum is the Great Arcanum.

'And as Moses lifted up the serpent in the wilderness, so must the Son of Man be lifted up.' (John 3:14). Those who incarnate him lift him up and raise him up from the dead within themselves.

'Truly, truly, I say to you, we speak of what we know, and bear witness to what we have seen; but you do not receive our testimony.' (John 3:11). Our Divine Saviour testifies to what He saw and experienced for himself. Jesus is a child of the Water and of the Fire. The Mother of the Word is always a woman. *'And no one has ascended into heaven, except the one who descended from heaven, the Son of Man who is in heaven.'* (John 3:13). We must dissolve the I. The I did not come from heaven. It cannot ascend into heaven. Only the Son of Man ascends into heaven, because he descended from heaven.

Everything exists through the Word. Everything is sustained through the Word.

The five vowels, I.E.O.U.A,. resound like a miraculous harp of the infinite cosmos in the flaming fire, in the impetuous air, in the raging waves and in the scented earth.

The vowel 'I' makes the frontal chakra vibrate. The vowel 'E' makes the laryngeal chakra vibrate. The vowel 'O' makes the chakra of the heart vibrate. The vowel 'U' makes the chakra of the solar plexus vibrate. The vowel 'A' makes the lung chakras vibrate.

All theses chakras, discs, or magnetic wheels of the astral body are developed and unfolded by vocalizing for an hour every day. Prana, life, must be inhaled through the nostrils, and

46

then it must be exhaled through the mouth as we vocalize. Each vowel has its own great power. The sound of every vowel has to be prolonged and sustained in order to awaken the chakras.

When we dwelt in Eden, all these sounds of the five vowels vibrated in our organism. Now we must awaken again these miraculous sounds of nature in all the chakras of our astral body. In Arcadia, in those ancient times of nature, we were paradisiacal men. Unfortunately the Lyre of Orpheus fell on the pavement of the temple broken into pieces.

Now we must pray, meditate, transmute and vocalize so that the Phoenix Bird can rise from its own ashes.

CHAPTER 11

The Church of Philadelphia

In every exquisite note of the piano, in every melody of Nirvana, the Church of Philadelphia shines full of mystical joy. When the sacred fire opens the Church of Philadelphia, the frontal chakra awakens. This chakra is situated between the two eyebrows. Mystics are filled with ecstasy when they see this lotus flower in their cavernous plexuses.

Amidst the sublime charms of the starry night the immaculate lotus of the brow resembles a love poem.

This beautiful lotus flower has its root in the pituitary gland. The frontal chakra shines with the immaculate colours of the romantic full moon nights. The frontal chakra has indeed many divine splendours, but its fundamental petals are only two.

The total and complete development of the frontal chakra means supreme beatitude and absolute liberation. The frontal chakra has eight major powers and thirty-six minor ones.

The frontal chakra makes us clairvoyant. Clairvoyants must have a child's mind. When clairvoyants allow the ego to be the translator of their visions, then they become slanderers.

Clairvoyants must be as simple and humble as the timid and scented little flower of the starry night. Clairvoyants must be like a garden sealed with seven seals. True clairvoyants never say that they are clairvoyant. True clairvoyants must be humble and modest. Clairvoyants must learn to see in the absence of the I. Seeing without translating. Seeing without judging.

The frontal chakra develops through deep inner meditation.

'And to the (atomic) *angel of the church in Philadelphia write: "These are the words of the one who is holy and true, who has the key of David, who opens and no one will shut, who shuts and no one opens.'* (Rev. 3:7).

The key of David is the key to every man's inner temple. We must build the temple on the living rock. The key to the temple is the key to the Ark of Science. That key is the A.Z.F. Arcanum. The Son of Man opens and no one can shut, and shuts and no one opens.

Do not throw stones from the interior of the temple. Do not use clairvoyance to hurt your fellow human beings. Have piety for those who suffer. Have piety for those who cry. Do not hurt them. Love them. Do not turn the temple into a den of merchants.

'"I know your works. Behold, I have set before you an open door (the door of the frontal chakra), *which no one is able to shut. I know that you have but little power, and yet you have kept my word and have not denied my name. Behold, I will make those of the synagogue of Satan who say that they are Jews and are not, but lie. Behold, I will make them come and bow down before your feet, and learn that I have loved you.'* (Rev. 3:8-9).

Real Jews are only the children of the lion of the tribe of Judah (the Christified Masters).

Those who say that they are Jews (Enlightened Masters) and are not, then they lie.

Those people belong indeed to the synagogue of Satan. Those people cannot enter the temple of Philadelphia.

When a clairvoyant is a black magician, his frontal chakra is then controlled by that woman called Jezebel (who calls herself a prophetess). Black magicians have dark clairvoyance .

The black magician's frontal chakra works only in the abyss. In the atomic hells of nature the adepts of of the shadow take the appearance of masters, pretending to be friends of the Masters, in order to do horrible things.

When the clairvoyant of Jezebel contact those disguised adepts of of the shadow, then in fact they become slanderers of their fellow human beings.

True enlightened clairvoyants are not capable of slandering their fellow human beings. Enlightened clairvoyants see in the absence of the I. Enlightened clairvoyants use their faculties with the utmost wisdom to advise and help their fellow human beings.

Jezebel has to be decapitated. We have to bring clairvoyance into the service of the Immolated Lamb. We have to prophesy with wisdom.

'*"Because you have kept my word of patient endurance, I will keep you from the hour of temptation, which is coming on the whole world, to try those who dwell on the earth.* (We are already in the hour of the great temptation). *I am coming soon. Hold fast what you have* (the fire) *so that no one may seize your crown.'* (Do not let Satan take it away from you). (Rev. 3:10-11). Do not waste the sacred wine. Be chaste.

'*"He who conquers, I will make him a pillar in the temple of my God. He will never go out of it, and I will write on him the name of my God and the name of the city of my God, the new Jerusalem, which comes down out of heaven from my God, and my own new name. He who has an ear, let him hear what the spirit says to the churches."'* (Rev. 3:12-13).

At our ascent towards the higher worlds, the sixth sense, divine clairvoyance, awakens.

And I will write on him, on his forehead, the name of the Lamb, and the name of the New Jerusalem above (the higher worlds), where we are received with palms and praises and festivals, the moment we free ourselves from the four bodies of sin.

And the New Jerusalem comes down out of heaven from my God, attired as a wife to receive her husband.

51

CHAPTER 12

The Church of Laodicea

When the igneous serpent of our magical powers reaches the pineal gland, situated in the brain, then the Church of Laodicea opens.

The pineal gland is situated in the upper part of the brain, and is the queen of the glands. Between the pituitary and pineal glands there is an very subtle tiny duct, which has disappeared in corpses. The fire has to go through that tiny duct on its way to the forehead. Then the fire goes down to the root of the nose. There, there is indeed a special magnetic field where the atom of the Father dwells. When we aspire to the Great Light, then we inhale billions of aspiring atoms that come into our organism through our nostrils down to the magnetic field of the root of the nose, where the atom of the Father is. The sexual glands and the pineal gland are closely correlated. The potency of the pineal gland depends on a person's sexual potency.

In the pineal gland is the atom of the Holy Spirit. In the pituitary gland is the atom of the Son. In the magnetic field of the root of the nose is the atom of the Father. The pineal gland is only five millimetres in diameter, and is surrounded by fine sand. The lotus of the pineal gland has one thousand petals that shine forming the crown of the saints. All the glory of the inner zodiac shines in the crown of the saints. In the microcosm-man there is a real shining and sparkling atomic zodiac. That is the shining halo around the heads of the saints.

As above, so below. The zodiac of the starry skies is governed by twenty-four elders.

Man-zodiac is also governed by twenty-four atomic gods who have their thrones in the brain. The aura of the twenty-four atomic gods sparkles in the crown of the saints.

Up there, in the starry skies, are the seven spirits before the throne of the Lamb. Down here, in the microcosm man, are the seven atomic angels who govern the Seven Churches of the spinal cord. *As above, so below.*

The pineal gland is the window of Brahma, the eye of diamond, the eye of poly-voyance. Intuitive sight, the eye of the Spirit, resides in this chakra. This resplendent and divine chakra is associated to the crown of thorns that makes the temples of all Christified Masters bleed.

With this chakra we can study the divine wisdom of Nirvana.

This chakra allows us to see and know instantaneously. Seeing with the eye of diamond means going spiritually to the place that we are seeing. Whoever has developed the coronal chakra can leave all his or her inner vehicles instantly every time he or she wants to. When the Intimate functions without vehicles of any kind in the world of the mist of fire, then we attain perfect ecstasy. When the fire reaches the atom of the Father, the first initiation of fire takes place.

The epiphysis and hypophysis glands (the pineal and pituitary glands) have each its own radiation, its own aura. When these two glandular auras mix together, then a jet of light goes out through the door of the frontal chakra.

When the initiate reaches these esoteric heights, he or she receives Initiation. The initiate has to ascend the seven degrees of power of the fire. The pentagonal star shines brightly with immaculate whiteness on the frontal chakra of the great initiates.

Some initiates rise in the fire and others rise in the light. We first rise in the fire, and then in the light.

As we aspire to the Light, millions of aspiring atoms reach the magnetic field of our nose, and then they go down to our heart. The Nous atom is in the heart.

That atom governs all the atoms in our organism. The Master atom is in our seminal system. With the practice of Sexual Alchemy that atom ascends to the brain to teach us the wisdom of nature.

All who reach the fifth initiation of greater mysteries become elder brothers of humanity.

Before you can arrive at the Valley of Refuge, known as the Path of Pure Knowledge, you will have to sacrifice yourself for the sake of humanity. The fifth path is supreme love, supreme charity and supreme obedience to the Father.

When the sacred serpent goes through that brain centre where the frontal fontanel of the newborn children is, then one part of the fire pours out onto the outer world. In those instants the whole aura shines full of fire, and the immaculate and divine white dove of the Holy Spirit comes into us. All the inner vehicles of the initiate must be crucified and stigmatized in the Golgotha of supreme sacrifice. In the brain is the Golgotha of the Father. We have to ascend to Golgotha carrying the cross on our shoulders.

The Twenty-Four Elders throw their crowns at the feet of the Lamb. Those who open the Church of Laodicea must cast their crowns humbly at the feet of the Lamb.

With the practice of inner meditation, the shining one-thousand-petalled lotus develops and unfolds.

You who cast your crown at the feet of the Lamb, remember that anyone who wants to attain mystical science has to deny and detach himself from five things: First, from the human passions, distractions and vices of the multitudes. Second, from the vain and transitory things of the world. Third, from the occult powers themselves. Having them in abundance, be as one who does not have them. Fourth, detach from yourself. Convince yourself that however exalted and magnificent your inner God may be, you are just the shadow of your God, a sinful shadow that must be annihilated. The fifth is: resolve to die.

Do not aspire to immortalize your I. Resolve to die completely, because you are just a poor sinful shadow. Then you will disappear into your inner God, and only the Son of Man will be left dwelling in your christified soul. You who have opened the Seven Churches, remember that occult powers are very divine, but dangerous.

If we do not dissolve the I, it happens that the I, armed with all these powers, wants to do something, and wishes to be great and powerful. Those initiates who become attached to magical powers move out of humility and Nothing, and fall into the abyss of perdition.

If you want to incarnate the Lamb, remember your own misery at every instant. It is through that Nothing and through the recognition of your own sin and misery that your God, who is awaiting, can perform wonders and prodigies within yourself.

Fast, pray, wear sackcloth and ashes, and do a great deal of penance. Never tell your sacred visions to anyone. Remember that Jezebel (who calls herself a prophetess) revels telling to people about all her visions.

You who throw your crown at the feet of the Lamb, learn to be quiet.

Never talk about the initiations of the Well-Beloved One. Those intimate matters about Initiation are very sacred.

The Well-Beloved One may be full of initiations and powers, but you are just a poor sinful shadow. It is urgent that you attain the annihilation of your I.

Never say, 'I have such-and-such an initiation, or so-and-so has such-and-such an initiation,' because your I has never received any initiations. Initiations are very sacred.

Only the Intimate is the one receiving initiations and degrees and festivals. Initiations are for the Intimate. You are just a shadow that must be annihilated.

'*And to the* (atomic) *angel of the church in Laodicea write: "These are the words of the Amen, the faithful and true witness, the beginning of God's creation. I know your works: you are neither cold nor hot. I wish that you were either cold or hot! So, because you are lukewarm, and neither cold nor hot, I will spew you out of my mouth.*' (Rev. 3:14-16).

Woe to those who are lukewarm! Lukewarm people cannot enter indeed into the secret path. Lukewarm people are parasites of nature. Very often a great sinner is closer to redemption than a lukewarm devotee. '*I will spew lukewarm people out of my mouth.*'

Lukewarm people say indeed, '*I am rich* (I am full of science, etc.), *I have prospered, and I need nothing*'; *not knowing that you are wretched, pitiable, poor, blind and naked. Therefore I counsel you to buy from me gold refined by fire* (through the sexual fire we must transmute the lead of the personality into the most pure gold of the Divine Spirit), *so that you may be rich* (spiritually), *and white garments to clothe you and to keep the shame of your nakedness from being seen, and salve to anoint your eyes, so that you may see.*' (Rev. 3:17-18).

The eye salve of chastity is the *Prima Materia* of the Great Work. That holy salve opens our eye of poly-voyance. The potency of the pineal gland depends on a person's sexual potency.

'"*I reprove and chasten those whom I love. So be zealous* (watchful) *and repent. Behold, I stand at the door and knock. If anyone hears my voice and opens the door* (the pineal gland is the door of the soul), *I will come in to him and eat with him, and he with me.*' (Rev. 3:19-20). The Lamb comes into us through the door of the pineal gland.

When the Lamb comes into the soul, he is transformed into it and it into Him. Then we raise up the Son of Man within ourselves.

'"*To him who conquers, I will grant to sit with me on my throne, as I myself conquered and sat down with my Father on his throne.*"' (Rev. 3:21). The soul mixed with the Lamb is the

57

Son of Man who sits on his throne. The Son of Man is a conqueror. He conquered Satan. He has the right to sit on the Throne of the Father, because the Son is One with the Father, and the Father is One with the Son. *'He who has an ear, let him hear what the Spirit says to the churches.'* (Rev. 3:22).

The Lamb must come into the Spirit (the Intimate) and into the soul, and into the body of man.

You who throw your crown at the feet of the Lamb, remember that you must build your temple on the living stone, so that the Lamb can come in to eat with you.

The Temple of Wisdom has seven pillars of living fire.

If you want Initiation, write it on a rod.

Only with INRI will you be able to arrive at the Golgotha of the Father.

CHAPTER 13

The Jinas States

*A*s *above, so below.* What is infinitely small is analogous to what is infinitely big. An atom is a complete solar system in miniature.

There exists the Heavenly Jerusalem in the macrocosm. There exists the Heavenly Jerusalem in the microcosm-man.

There will be a new heaven and a new earth. That is the future Heavenly Jerusalem of the macrocosm.

When a man becomes christified, he also becomes the new Heavenly Jerusalem of the microcosm. *As above, so below.* That is the law.

The New Jerusalem — both in the macrocosm and in the microcosm — comes down from the higher worlds, and is full of terribly divine powers.

The New Jerusalem — both in the future planet earth and in the planet man — is illuminated by the Immolated Lamb.

The purified planet of the future plus the inner bodies of the planet are the future Heavenly Jerusalem in the macrocosm.

Man's christified body plus his christified inner bodies constitute the Heavenly Jerusalem of the microcosm-man.

Everything that happens in the planet earth repeats itself in the planet man. Everything that happens in the Heavenly Jerusalem of the macrocosm repeats itself in the Heavenly Jerusalem of the microcosm-man. *As above, so below.*

In the Heavenly Jerusalem of the future planet earth, only christified souls will dwell. In the Heavenly Jerusalem of the human body, only the initiate's christified soul dwells.

The human body of a christified master is the Heavenly Jerusalem of the microcosm. That christic body is full of terrible powers.

The eight major powers of the mystic are the following:

First: *Anima*. The power to reduce the size of one's physical body to the size of an atom.

Second: *Mahima*. The power to enlarge oneself to the point of being able to touch the sun and the moon with one's hands.

Third: *Laghima*. The power to turn one's body as light as a feather. With this power we can float in the air with our body.

Fourth: *Gharima*. The power to increase the weight of the body at will, to the point of becoming as heavy as a mountain.

Fifth: *Prapti*. Prophecy, clairvoyance, sacred ear, psychometry, telepathy, intuition, the power to understand the language of animals, as Apollonius Thianeus and Francis of Assisi did. The latter could even talk to animals in the woods.

Sixth: *Prakanya*. The power allowing mystics to plunge into water and even live under the waters without being harmed.

The Great Guru-Deva Sivananda tells us the case of Swami Trilinga of Benares (India), who used to live for six months under the waters of the Ganges.

Seventh: *Vasitwan*. The power with which mystics can control the fiercest animals. The power to pronounce words that numb and enchant poisonous snakes.

Eighth: *Ishatwan*. The power allowing saints to raise the dead. The adept who has reached this point is a liberated one, a Lord of the living and of the dead.

All those who are walking in the path of Christification must develop these eight powers. These powers of the Heavenly

Jerusalem are obtained and conquered with the practice of inner meditation (provided that there is absolute chastity).

When the human body becomes the Heavenly Jerusalem, it is a marvellous christic body.

PRACTICE

1. Let the mystic lie in bed peacefully.

2. Let the mystic ask the Inner Lamb for the assistance of an angel specialized in the Jinas states.

3. Entreat the angel and the Immolated Lamb that they take you to the higher worlds with your physical body.

4. We Brothers of the Temple advise you to invoke Angel Harpocrates, who is a specialist in the Jinas states. Pray to the Lamb. Entreat him that Harpocrates be sent to you.

5. Remove all thoughts from your mind (empty your mind). It is necessary that you have a still and calm mind.

6. Induce sleep on you. Fall slightly asleep thinking of nothing.

7. Get up from your bed and leave your bedroom keeping your sleep as if it was a precious treasure.

If the practice has been done properly, your body will go into the Jinas state; it will plunge into the suprasensible worlds.

A body in the Jinas state can float in the air (Laghima), or plunge into the waters (Prakanya), or go through fire without being burnt, or be reduced to the size of an atom (Anima), or be enlarged to the point of being able to touch the sun and the moon with one's hands (Mahima).

A body plunged into the suprasensible worlds is subjected to the laws of those worlds. Then it is plastic, elastic; it can change its shape, decrease its weight (Laghima), or increase its weight (Gharima) at will.

61

The yogi of Benares who remained submerged for six months under the waters could do it because he first put his body in the Jinas state.

Some devotees who were doing meditation practices for going into the Jinas state suddenly felt as if they were very fat. They had the sensation of being swelling like balloons.

If those devotees would have got up from their beds in those precise instants, then they would have had the joy of going into the Jinas state.

When Jesus walked on the waters of the Sea of Galilee, his body was in the Jinas state.

Peter was able to release himself from his shackles and get out of prison thanks to an angel who helped him to put his body in the Jinas state.

The Heavenly Jerusalem of the microcosm-man is full of tremendous divine powers.

With the practice of inner meditation you will be able to develop the eight great mystical powers and you will become living models of the future Heavenly Jerusalem.

A great deal of patience and many years of practice are needed to educate, develop and strengthen the eight great mystical powers.

Devotees must be patient in these Jinas practices. It is necessary to persevere for days, months and years until the eight great mystical powers are completely educated, developed and strengthened. In the Jinas state we have power over nature with the powers of the Seven Churches.

What is needed is faith, tenacity, patience, chastity, charity and supreme love for humanity. These virtues are essential. In this way you will be able to develop the eight mystical powers of your own Heavenly Jerusalem. Those eight mystical powers belong to the Seven Churches.

Those who grow weary; those who are unsteady; those who commit adultery with Jezebel (who calls herself a prophetess)

The Jinas States

will never obtain the eight mystical powers of the saints.

In the Jinas state we exercise the perfect priesthood of the Seven Churches. Every man who attains Christification becomes a living exponent, a living example, of the future Jerusalem.

When all the inner vehicles of a man are christified and stigmatized, they shine with the glory of the Lamb. That is indeed the Holy Tabernacle of God with men. The Lord dwells in his Holy Tabernacle. That is the Heavenly Jerusalem, endowed with terribly divine powers. And the Heavenly Jerusalem has no need of sun or moon to shine on it, because the immaculate light of the Eternal illuminates it, and the Lamb is its luminary.

The Holy Eight is the sign of infinity. The two witnesses of the Book of Revelation coil around the spinal cord forming the Holy Eight. All the mystical powers of the Heavenly Jerusalem of the microcosm-man come from that Holy Eight. Now the devotees will understand the reason why we speak about the eight mystical ineffable powers.

'The wall of the city is one hundred and forty-four cubits, by a man's measure, that is, an angel's.' (Rev. 21:17) 1+4+4=9. We must go down to the Ninth Sphere (sex) to work with the water and the fire, origin of worlds, beasts, men and gods. Every genuine white initiation begins there.

The Son of Man is born of water and fire. 'And the one who talked to me had a measuring rod of gold to measure the city and its gates and walls.' (Rev. 21:15). That rod of gold is the spinal cord. The seven degrees of the power of the fire ascend along it. Take up your rod so that you can exercise the priesthood of the saints.

You can become early citizens of the future Jerusalem.

Just as the dawn breaks in the east shortly before sunrise, bringing joy to birds, who then begin to fill the wood with the sweetness of their moving songs; so the dawn of the Eternal breaks with some living examples of what the New Jerusalem will be before the arrival of the ineffable future Jerusalem.

63

Develop your inner powers. Do not covet powers. Do not desire powers. Cultivate the lotus flowers with an unselfish love. Cultivate your precious, inner and delicate garden, just as the poor gardener cultivates his garden.

When your lotus flowers shine, remember that all your powers are just miserable candles shining like glow-worms in the presence of the resplendent sun of your Immolated Lamb.

You are not the Master. You are only the sinful shadow of him who has never sinned. Remember that only your Inner Lamb is the Master.

Remember that although your Inner God is a hierarch of fire, you, poor worm, are only a man, and as such you will be always judged.

Your Inner Lamb may be a planetary God; but you, poor worm of the mud, remember, and do not forget, that you are only the shadow of your God. Poor sinful shadow!

Do not say, I am God so-and-so, or I am Master so-and-so, because you are just a shadow that must be resolved to die decapitated so as not to be an obstacle for your Inner God. It is necessary that you attain supreme humility.

PART TWO

THE SEALED SCROLL

'IN OMNIBUS DEBEMUS SUBICERE VOLUNTATEM
NOSTRAM VOLUNTATIS DIVINAE'

CHAPTER 14

The Throne in Heaven

'*After this I looked, and behold, in heaven there was an open door!* (The door of the pineal gland). *And the first voice which I had heard speaking to me like a trumpet, said, "Come up here, and I will show you what must take place after this." At once I was in the Spirit, and there in heaven stood a throne, with one seated on the throne!* (The Lamb). *And the one who sat there appeared like jasper and carnelian.* (The Son of Man is a child of the living stone, and all the Masters are children of the precious stones of the Temple. The cubic stone of Jesod symbolizes sex). *And around the throne was a rainbow that looked like an emerald.* (The halo of wisdom. The Son of Man is the spirit of wisdom). *Around the throne were twenty-four thrones, and seated on the thrones were twenty-four elders* (the twenty-four elders who govern the Zodiac), *dressed in white garments, with golden crowns on their heads. From the throne issue flashes of lightning, and voices and peals of thunder, and before the throne burn seven torches of fire, which are the seven spirits of God.*' (Rev. 4: 1-5).

The twenty-four elders exist in the macrocosm and in the microcosm, above and below, in the firmament of heaven and in man's atomic firmament.

The seven spirits before the throne exist above and below, in the firmament of heaven and in man's atomic firmament. As above, so below.

67

Just as there is a zodiac in heaven, so there is also a living zodiac on earth. That zodiac is man.

'*And in front of the throne* (both in heaven and in man) *there was something like a sea of glass, like crystal* (the *ens seminis*). *And around the throne, on each side of the throne* (the throne that is above and below, in the universe and in man), *were four living creatures, full of eyes in front and behind.* (The four living creatures that symbolize the whole science of the Great Arcanum). (Rev. 4:6).

'*And the first living creature was like a lion* (the sacred fire); *the second living creature was like an ox* (the salt, that is, matter); *the third living creature had a face of a man* (the mercury of secret philosophy, the *ens seminis*), *and the fourth living creature was like a flying eagle.* (The flying eagle symbolizes the element of air). (Rev. 4:7).

The philosophical fire must be sought in the *ens seminis*. At first, this fire is just a dry and earthly exhalation that is mixed with the seminal vapours. When the priest learns to withdraw from the altar without wasting a single drop of the sacred wine, then that dry and earthly exhalation is transmuted into the terrible thunderbolt of Kundalini. When we reach this point, we receive the flaming sword.

When the *ens seminis* is fertilized by the fire, it becomes the master and regenerator of man. The fire feeds on the vital air, prana or universal life. The fire, through its being inhaled and exhaled for so long during the supreme ecstasy of love, becomes indeed the terrible thunderbolt that opens the Seven Churches as it ascends along the spinal canal.

We have to decapitate the I with the flaming sword of cosmic justice.

'*And the four living creatures* (of sexual alchemy), *each of them with six wings, were full of eyes all around and within, and day and night they never cease to sing, "Holy, holy, holy is the Lord God Almighty, who was and is and is to come." '* (Rev. 4:8).

This is the terrible Arcanum 6 of the Tarot. Remember that when Moses strikes the philosopher's stone with his rod, the spring of pure water of life gushes out.

Man is the priest and woman is the altar. The sacred wine is the *ens seminis*, the pure water of life.

Remember Moses' copper serpent coiling around the Tau, that is, around the generating lingam. Remember, good devotee, the double tail of the serpent, forming the legs of the solar cock of the Abraxas. The whole object of the Great Work is to free ourselves from the enchanted rings of the seductive serpent; to tame it; to defeat it; to put our foot on its head and to lift it up along our spinal canal in order to open the Seven Churches.

The Arcanum 6 is the fight between the Spirit and the animal beast. The number six represents the fight between God and the devil, the antagonism between love and animal passion. The six wings of the four living creatures are full of eyes watching us above and below, in heaven and in the abyss.

'Woe to you, O Warrior, O Fighter, if your servant sinks!'

Do not spill the sacred wine of your temple.

'And whenever the living creatures give glory, honour and thanks to the one who is seated on the throne (within man and in the universe), *who lives for ever and ever* (the Lamb), *the twenty-four elders* (in the macrocosm and in the microcosm) *fall down before him who is seated on the throne and worship him who lives for ever and ever. They cast their crowns before the throne, singing, "You are worthy, our Lord and God, to receive glory and honour and power, for you created all things, and by your will they existed and were created."'* (Rev. 4:9-11).

The twenty-four elders of the Zodiac in heaven throw their crowns at the feet of the Lamb. This event repeats itself in the man-zodiac. The twenty-four atomic elders in the brain throw their crowns at the feet of the Lamb. *As above, so below.* Everything that happens in what is infinitely big repeats itself in what is infinitely small.

The Lamb is Perfect Multiple Unity. There are as many Lambs in heaven as men on earth. Every man has indeed his own Lamb.

The Lamb is not the Theosophical Septenary. The Lamb is the Logoic Ray from where the whole Theosophical Septenary emanates.

When the Intimate opens the Seven Churches, he must throw his crown at the feet of the Lamb. The Intimate is the Spirit, the Monad, the Being.

The Intimate is not the Lamb. The Intimate emanated from the Lamb.

When the initiate pronounces the terrible seventh word of Golgotha, he gives up his spirit to the Lamb, and exclaims, *'My Father, into your hands I commend my spirit.'* (Luke 23:46).

CHAPTER 15

The Sealed Scroll

Tonight we, the Brothers of the Temple, have suffered a great deal for that poor humanity which we adore so much. Tonight the sky is clothed with black and dense storm clouds.Tawny clouds lit up by flashes of lightning... There are thunderbolts, thunder-claps, storms, rain and very heavy hail.Tonight we all went in through the doors of the temple, filled with very great tribula-tion. We have suffered a great deal for the great orphan we love so much. Poor humanity! Poor mothers! Poor old people!

Some of us have lain on beds of deep pain.An apocalyptic drama is performed in the temple.

We brothers are simultaneously spectators and actors in this sacred drama. The priests tied together two things: a child and a scroll. The sealed scroll shines on the chest of the apocalyptic child. The ropes of thin and cruel hemp envelop the delicate and tender body of the beautiful child of anguish and pain. The cruel strings are over the sealed scroll. The scroll is on the immacu-late chest of the child. That child is our much beloved son. We entreated, cried, begged for mercy, and then the child of anguish is set free, and the scroll is sealed with seven seals.

Now we open the scroll and with it we prophesy to a woman dressed in purple and scarlet. That woman is the great harlot whose number is 666, and with her all the kings of the earth have fornicated. The woman listens to us and says, 'I did not know that you could prophesy to me with that book.' We then said, 'We have come to prophesy and to teach with this book.'

71

We thus spoke to the woman dressed in purple and scarlet, and as we talk to her, the images of five mountains pass across our imagination. Those are the five races that have already been. Every race ends with a great cataclysm. Our fifth race will end soon.

'*And I saw in the right hand of the one seated on the throne a scroll written on the inside and on the back, sealed with seven seals.*' (Rev. 5:1).

'*And I saw a strong angel proclaiming with a loud voice, "Who is worthy to open the scroll and break its seals?" And no one in heaven or on earth or under the earth was able to open the scroll or to look into it.*' (Rev. 5:3). Only the Incarnated Lamb can indeed open that scroll.

'*And I wept a great deal because no one was found worthy to open the scroll or to look into it.*' (Rev. 5:4).

'*Then one of the elders said to me, "Do not weep. See, the lion of the tribe of Judah*' (the Word who is initiating the New Aquarian Era), *the root of David, has conquered* (the beast within himself), *so that he can open the scroll and its seven seals."*' (Rev. 5:5). Humanity, the Great Harlot, is ignorant of this.

'*Then I saw between the throne and the four living creatures and among the elders a Lamb standing as if it had been immolated, with seven horns and with seven eyes, which are the seven spirits of God sent out into all the earth,*' (in order to work in accordance with the Law). (Rev. 5:6).

'*And he went and took the scroll from the right hand of the one who was seated on the throne.*' (Rev. 5:7).

'*And when he had taken the scroll, the four living creatures and the twenty-four elders fell down before the Lamb, each holding a harp, and with golden bowls full of incense, which are the prayers of the saints. And they sang a new song, saying, "You are worthy to take the scroll and to open its seals, because you were immolated and with your blood you ransomed men for God from every tribe and tongue and people and nation.*' (Rev. 5: 8-9). Only the Lamb can indeed open the sealed scroll.

'*"And you have made them a kingdom and priests to our* (Inner) *God, and they will reign on earth."'* (Rev. 5:10). Our Inner God is really the king and the priest.

'*Then I looked, and I heard the voice of many angels around the throne* (that is in heaven and in the heart of man) *and the living creatures and the elders, numbering myriads of myriads and thousands of thousands, saying with a loud voice, "Worthy is the Lamb who was immolated, to receive power and wealth and wisdom and might and honour and glory and praise!" And I heard every creature in heaven and on earth and under the earth and in the sea, and all that is in them, saying, "To him who sits on the throne and to the Lamb be blessing and honour and glory and might for ever and ever!"'* (Rev. 5:11-13).

'*And the four living creatures* (of sexual alchemy) *said, "Amen!" And the twenty-four elders fell down and worshipped.'* (Rev. 5:14).

The Inner Lamb of every man is indeed absolutely perfect and worthy of all honour. We men are just poor shadows of sin. Some people say, 'I believe in *I want*, as well as in *I can* and in *I do*.' They call it to be positive. The reality is that these people are affirming Satan. The Lamb is not the I. The Lamb is not a 'higher I', still less a 'lower I'. When the Lamb says I Am, this has to be translated in this way: He Is, since He is the one who is speaking, and He is no man. The Lamb is devoid of any I, and of any mark of individuality, and of any trace of personality.

If your Inner God is the God of some sun, the god of some constellation, be still humbler because you are just a poor bodhisattva, a poor man who is more o less imperfect. Do not commit the sacrilege of saying, 'I am the god so-and-so, or the great Master so-and-so,' because you are not the Master. You are not the Lamb. You are just only a sinful shadow of the one who has never sinned. The I is composed of the atoms of the secret enemy. The I wants to stand out, to go up, to make itself noticed, to climb to the top of the ladder, etc. You, admit your misery, adore and praise the Lamb, vanish yourself, take refuge in Nothing,

73

because you are no one. Thus, through the path of supreme humility you will return to the innocence of Eden. Then your soul will disappear into the Lamb. The spark will return to the flame from where it went out. You are the spark; the Lamb is the flame.And in those days, when your soul has returned to the Lamb, multiply your watchfulness. Remember that the I sprouts again as weed. Only the Lamb is worthy of all praise and honour and glory.

Do not divide yourself into two I's, one higher and the other lower. There is only one I. What is called 'higher I' is just a refined concept of Satan, a sophism of the I.

Desire nothing. Kill every desire to live. Remember that the I feeds on every desire. Kiss the feet of the leper. Wipe away the tears of your worst enemies. Do not hurt anyone with your speech. Seek no refuge. Resolve to die in all the planes of cosmic consciousness. Give your goods to the poor. Give your last drop of blood for the poor suffering humanity. Renounce all happiness and then the Immolated Lamb will enter your soul. He will make his dwelling place in your soul.

Some philosophers affirm that the Christ brought us the doctrine of the I because he said, 'I am the way, the truth and the life.' (John 14:6). Certainly the Lamb said, 'I am'. Only the Lamb can say I Am. The Lamb said that, but we (poor shadows of sin) cannot say that. Because we are not the Lamb. The exact and axiomatic translation of that I Am, uttered by the Lamb, is really the following, 'He Is the way, the truth and the life.' He said that, because *He Is* said that. We did not say that, He, He, He said that.He lives in the unknown depths of our being. He Is the way, the truth and the life. He transcends any concept of I, of individuality, and any trace of personality.The Lamb who was immolated is indeed worthy to receive power, and riches, and wisdom, and strength, and honour, and glory, and blessing. He is the only one worthy to open the scroll and to break its seals.

The Lamb is our divine Augoides. The only one that is truly great and divine is the Immolated Lamb.

CHAPTER 16

The Seven Seals

'*T*hen I saw the Lamb open one of the seven seals, and I heard one of the four living creatures (of the Great Arcanum) say, as with a voice of thunder, "Come!"' (Rev. 6:1).

'And I saw, and behold, a white horse (the white race). *Its rider had a bow, and a crown was given to him, and he went out conquering and to conquer.'* (Rev. 6:2). The white race conquered Japan, and has many illustrations against Japan.

'When he opened the second seal, I heard the second living creature (of the Great Arcanum) *say, "Come!" And out came another horse, bright red* (the Atlantean red race from which the redskins of the United States of America are descended). *Its rider* (Uncle Sam) *was permitted to take peace from the earth, so that men should kill one another, and he was given a great sword.'* (Rev. 6:3-4).

That red horse, with its ruffled hirsute mane and silvery hooves, is currently eating in the Augean Stables peacefully.

The spirited redskin steed, agile and swift, reminds us of the hardened Atlantean race, whose last scions, noble and strong, were destroyed by the Yankee.

The blond citizens of the United States of America carry in their veins the red blood of the old warriors, whose real trunk originated in the Atlantean continent. In this year 1958 (20th century), the red horse is eating peacefully and the citizens of the United States are getting ready for the atomic war.

Soon the storm will break in the United States. The hurricane will howl horribly in the United States. The sky will be filled with black storm clouds, and there will be many wails, tears and very great tribulation.

'And when he opened the third seal, I heard the third living creature (of the Great Arcanum) *say, "Come!" And I saw, and behold, a black horse* (the black race, and every dark-skinned race, such as Hindustanis, Africans, etc. This horse also represents honest work). *And its rider* (the black or dark-skinned races, the Arabs, Hindustanis, etc.) *held a pair of scales in his hand* (slavery).' (Rev. 6:5).

'And I heard what seemed to be a voice in the middle of the four living creatures saying, "A quart of wheat for a denarius, and three quarts of barley for a denarius, but do not harm the oil and the wine!"' (Rev. 6:6).

This is hard work. This is hard struggling for the daily bread. And the initiates want peace and say, 'Do not harm the sacred wine and the oil of pure gold that feeds the fire in the lampstand.'

Work in peace. Fight for peace. *'Love one another as I have loved you.'* And look after the wine and the oil, so that you soul can marry the Lamb. However, the dwellers of the earth only want war.

'And when he opened the fourth seal, I heard the voice of the fourth living creature (of the Great Arcanum) *say, "Come!" And I saw, and behold, a yellow horse* (the yellow race). *And the name of its rider* (the Chinese) *was Death, and Hades followed him, and they were given power over a fourth of the earth to kill with sword, famine and pestilence, and by the* (human) *wild beasts of the earth.'* (Rev. 6: 7-8).

The war between the East and the West will be horrible, and China will kill millions of human beings. The Chinese danger is terrifying. The Chinese horse draws hell and death behind itself. Never will be there a more terrible danger.

The Chinese army is terribly powerful, and is armed with all kinds of deadly weapons.

The times of the end have already come, and the war between the East and the West is inevitable.

The yellow horse is neighing, agile and full of great anger, and it draws hell and death behind itself.

'And when he opened the fifth seal, I saw under the altar the souls of those who had been killed because of the word of God and the testimony they had given. They cried out with a loud voice, "O Sovereign Lord, holy and true, how long will it be before you judge and avenge our blood on those who dwell on the earth?"' (In accordance with Karmic Law). (Rev. 6:9-10).

The dwellers of the earth have killed the prophets and hate the Eternal.

'Then they were each given a white robe, and they were told to rest a little longer, until the number of their fellow-servants and their brothers (initiates) *should be complete, who were to be killed as they themselves had been* (for the word of the Lord).' (Rev. 6:11).

'And when he opened the sixth seal, I looked, and behold, there was a great earthquake, and the sun became black as sackcloth, and the full moon became like blood.' (Rev. 6:12).

Radioactive particles from nuclear explosions will deeply damage the upper zones of the earth's atmosphere. Those upper zones are the supreme filter of the solar rays. When that filter has been completely damaged by atomic explosions, then it will no longer be able to analyze and break up the solar rays into light and fire. The result will be that we will see the sun black as sackcloth.

Men will disembark on the moon. The conquest of the moon is inevitable. The vultures of war are conquering the moon, and the whole moon will become as blood. There will be earthquakes everywhere, darkness, famine, unknown diseases, blasphemies and very great tribulation. Atomic explosions will cause all those great calamities.

The times of the end have already come. Woe! Woe! Woe! to those who, as in the days of Noah, ate and drank and gave in marriage, saying, 'We still have time to enjoy.'

Woe to the dwellers of the earth! The times of the end have already come.

Atomic explosions will bring plagues, earthquakes, famine, seaquakes and terrible cataclysms. There will be a frightful trepidation in the sound of the sea and monstrous waves never seen before. There will be wars to the death, and the yellow horse will draw hell and death behind itself.

The beginning of the end has already begun.

However, all these calamities are just the warning, the preface, the prelude to the final event.

Men are building again the Tower of Babel. The moon is the top end of this tower. Every enlightened clairvoyant can see the Tower of Babel in the higher worlds. A hallow tower made of fragile glass, a betrayal of the Eternal, which will be soon shattered.

The ships of Babylon the Great, the mother of all fornication and abominations of the earth, go up and down through that fragile and hallow tower that is devoid of any divine wisdom.

This time, the Tower of Babel is represented by the hallow, superficial and vain science of the materialistic scientists.

God will confuse their tongues, and the Tower of Babel will be stricken down by the terrible thunderbolt of Cosmic Justice.

The fragile and hallow tower, devoid of any spirituality, nowadays as it happened in the past, is threatening again the starry skies.

The atheistic enemies of the Eternal want to storm the sky and conquer other worlds of space. Soon they will be fatally wounded.

In sacred space, where only countless worlds seethe and pal-
pitate, the terror of love and law reigns. Interplanetary journeys
are only for the divine humanities of starry space. The man of
the earth is still not worthy to travel into starry space. Let us
place a monkey in a laboratory and let us observe what happens
there.

When men conquer the moon. When the atheistic enemies of
the Eternal desecrate sacred space. When the scientists of the
Great Babylon, full of pride and arrogance, prepare the conquest of other worlds, then it is the end.

The Tower of Babel will fall stricken down, and of all this
Great Babylon there will not be left one stone upon another.

A world is coming to us. It is now approaching the earth. Woe
to the dwellers of the earth!

The day of the Lord (the New Aquarian Era) is nearly here,
and that world that is approaching will go through the earth's
atmosphere; it will ignite in blazing fire, and when it falls to the
earth, it will burn everything that is alive with fire, and there
will be such a great earthquake as has never been before since
men exist on the earth.

'*And the stars of the sky* (the great geniuses of the Tower of
Babel, the great luminaries of the intellectual firmament, the
great lords of the Great Babylon) *fell to the earth as the fig tree
drops its winter fruit when shaken by a gale.*' (Rev. 6:13).

The ears of materialistic science grew ripe, and man will reap
the fruits of desire. Now he will gather the result of this civilization without God and without law.

'*And the sky vanished like a scroll that is rolled up* (with the
planetary collision), *and every mountain and island was removed from its place.*' (Rev. 6:14). The new planetary mass,
mixed with the earth's mass, will form a new world. There will
be new skies and a new earth for the future sixth great race.

'*Then the kings of the earth, the princes, the generals, the
rich, the strong, and everyone, slave and free* (after their death

79

and in their astral bodies), *hid in the caves and among the rocks of the mountains* (being horrified and surprised at a cataclysm which they do not expect, and which they do not even remotely suspect).' (Rev. 6:15).

'*Calling to the mountains and rocks, "Fall on us and hide us from the face of the one who is seated on the throne and from the wrath* (justice) *of the Lamb."*' (Rev. 6:16).

'*For the great day of their wrath has come, and who can stand before it?*' (Rev. 6:17).

Only those who have built the church of the Lamb on the living rock, on sex, will be indeed able to stand.

Those who built their church on the sand of theories will tumble down to the abyss, to the sunken worlds, to the atomic hells of great nature. Those are the lost ones.

In those days only the righteous will be secretly saved. Those who raised the serpent on the rod, as Moses did in the desert. The seedbed for the future sixth great race will come out of them.

The times of the end have already come, and we are in them. '*Many are called but few are chosen.*' (Matthew 20:16).

The Great Master said, '*Out of one thousand men who seek me, one finds me. Out of one thousand who find me, one follows me. Out of one thousand who follow me, one is mine.*'

CHAPTER 17

The Four Angels

In the supreme instant of ecstasy we, the Brothers, have gone in through the doors of the Temple of Jerusalem. In this valley of sorrows, only the Wailing Wall remains. Yet, the temple still exists in the higher worlds. We walked full of pain through its courts and corridors.

We gazed at its olympic columns with their beautiful capitals, and its chambers, and its vessels of gold and silver, and its purples, and its kneelers.

The glory of the Lord Jehovah no longer shines in the Holy of Holies of the Temple. The sanctuary has been devastated. The sanctuary has been desecrated.

No longer is there the Ark of Science, with its sacred, terribly divine cherubim coupled together. Now in the Holy of Holies of the Temple we only see the Lord of Anguish.

His sacred image is there. An image that is alive. The image of the Adorable One is there, and the Jews laugh at Him, and they say, 'That is the one who dreamt that he was the promised Messiah and we do not believe in him.'

They are all laughing. The sanctuary has been desecrated. The veil of the temple was torn in two, because the sanctuary had already been desecrated. When the Christ was killed, the sanctuary was desecrated. We the Brothers of the Temple walked through its interior. The priests' court was full of sportsmen and merchants. Such is the way in which the sacred temple of

81

Jerusalem ended up. Humanity crucified the Christ and signed its own death sentence with innocent blood.

Nevertheless, infinite mercy gave us a little more time so that we could define ourselves either for Christ or for Jahve, either for the White Lodge or for the Black Lodge.

We all deserved to have been destroyed because of the dreadful and horrible sacrilege. The Christ murdered and the sanctuary desecrated. However, infinite mercy gave us a little more time so that we could study the doctrine of the Christ and choose the path.

'After this (the events that happened in Jerusalem) *I saw four angels standing at the four corners of the earth* (the four archivists of Karma, the four Devarajas), *holding back the four winds of the earth, so that no wind might blow on the earth or on the sea or against any tree.'* (Rev. 7:1). They rule the four winds and control the four points of the earth with the Law.

The prophet saw the four saints holding back the Law, holding back the four winds of the earth so that no wind could blow on the earth, or on the sea, or on any tree. The four saints held back the Law, the punishment that hangs over the head of the humanity that murdered the Christ. Infinite mercy gave us time to study the doctrine of the Lord and to return to the good way.

'Then I saw another angel ascending from the rising of the sun, having the seal of the living God (the Seal of Solomon), *and he called with a loud voice to the four angels who had been given power to harm the earth and the sea, saying, "Do not harm the earth or the sea or the trees, until we have marked the servants of our God with a seal on their foreheads."'* (Rev. 7:2-3).

The bodhisattva of the angel who has the seal of the living God in his hands is now reincarnated in this 20th century. He has a female body and is a marvellous specialist in the Jinas states. His sacred name must not be divulged.

This angel told us all the following truth: *'We are going to save the people in this street in ten days.'* We understood that he referred to the street of the righteous, one of the streets of the Great Babylon. The ten days symbolize the wheel of the ages, the wheel of reincarnation and Karma.

A period of time was needed so that people could study the doctrine of the Christ and define themselves either for Christ or for Jahve, either for the White Lodge or for the Black Lodge.

The servants of God were already sealed on their foreheads. The servants of Satan were also sealed on their foreheads. The times of the end have already come and we are in them. The ten days have already expired, and the times of the end have already come.

The Seal of Solomon is the supreme affirmation of the Lamb and the supreme denial of Satan. Hilarius IX said, *'Its two triangles, which love puts together or puts apart, are the shuttles with which the loom of God is woven and unwoven.'* The six points of the seal of the living God are male. The six deep recesses that are between one point and the next are female. All in all, this seal of the living God has twelve rays: six male and six female. These twelve rays chrystallize in the twelve constellations of the zodiac through sexual alchemy. These twelve zodiacal constellations are the twelve sons of Jacob. The whole of humanity is divided into twelve tribes: the twelve tribes of Israel.

Humanity is classified with the seal of the living God. Most of humanity has already received the mark of the beast on their foreheads and on their hands. A few received the sign of the Lamb on their foreheads.

'And I heard the number of those who were sealed, one hundred and forty-four thousand sealed, from every tribe of the sons of Israel.' (Rev. 7:4). By kabbalistically adding up the numbers among themselves we will get the number nine: 1+4+4=9. Nine is the Ninth Sphere (sex). Only those who have attained absolute chastity will be saved.

Today 5th September, 1958.

The great storm is drawing near. The sky is full of black and threatening clouds lit up by lightning. An icy breeze of death is blowing everywhere. We have all cried a great deal. We have all entreated a most awesome watchman and saint. We have begged him. We have proposed a deal to him in order to conjure the terrible storm that is hanging threateningly over the poor suffering humanity. We have asked for a key for conjuring the storm, but all has been in vain.

The times expired, and those who did not accept the doctrine of the Lord will sink into the abyss. Only the righteous will be saved: Those who have already received the sign of God on their foreheads, those who have attained supreme chastity. One hundred and forty-four thousand righteous ones will be saved. Only supreme chastity and supreme love towards the whole of suffering humanity can really achieve the divine miracle of our Christification.

We must kiss with supreme adoration the whip of the tormentor who hates us. We must purge our minds of all desire. We must watch the I in all the levels of consciousness. Many faithful and sincere devotees who attained chastity in this valley of tears turned out to be terrible fornicators in the world of the cosmic mind. Have you ever meditated on the danger of erotic images? Remember that you have a clever translator in your mind. That translator is your I.

The I betrays the devotees of the Path. The I creates mental effigies, living demons of the mental plane. In the mental world the devotees fornicate with those demons. Cinemas are real temples of black magic of the mental world. The mind creates living effigies, tempting demons that are absolutely identical to the erotic images which we have seen in the cinema, or in newspapers, or in pornographic magazines.

The I betrays us in other levels of consciousness. A simple erotic word turns into fornication in the mental world. An ironic word means violence in the mental plane.

We need to love and adore our worst enemies. We need to attain supreme chastity in all the levels of consciousness. We need to give even the last drop of our blood for this adorable humanity. Our lips must kiss the feet of those who hate us and curse us most. Our hands must be raised only to bless the enemy who spits at us and whips us.

The number of christified saints are one hundred and forty-four thousand. This means washing our feet in the waters of renunciation. This means supreme chastity, supreme sanctity and supreme love towards all the millions of beings who populate the world.

We have to go down to the Ninth Sphere in order to work with the fire and the water, origin of worlds, beasts, men and gods. Every genuine white initiation begins there. We must work with the A.Z.F. Arcanum. Only in that way is it possible to receive the sign of God on our foreheads.

'And I heard the number of those who were sealed, one hundred and forty-four thousand sealed, from every tribe of the sons of Israel. From the tribe of Judah twelve thousand sealed, from the tribe of Reuben twelve thousand, from the tribe of Gad twelve thousand, from the tribe of Asher twelve thousand, from the tribe of Naphtali twelve thousand, from the tribe of Manasseh twelve thousand, from the tribe of Simeon twelve thousand, from the tribe of Levi twelve thousand, from the tribe of Issachar twelve thousand, from the tribe of Zebulun twelve thousand, from the tribe of Joseph twelve thousand, from the tribe of Benjamin twelve thousand sealed.' (Rev. 7:4-8).

The whole of poor humanity is divided into twelve tribes. Every humanity develops and unfolds in the zodiacal womb. The zodiac is a womb in which humanity is gestated. These twelve zodiacal tribes can receive the sign of God on their foreheads only by practising the A.Z.F. Arcanum.

From every one of the twelve zodiacal tribes there are only twelve thousand sealed. Here is the Arcanum 12 of the Tarot. This Arcanum is represented by a man hanging from one of his feet.

His two hands tied behind his back together with his head form a triangle with its point down, and his two legs form a cross above the triangle. Here is the union of the cross with the triangle. This is sexual magic. This is the A.Z.F. Arcanum. This is the work completed — the living man who touches the earth only with his thought.

The whole science of sexual alchemy was engraved by Hermes on an Emerald [Table]. Here are the precepts referring to the Great Work:

'You shall separate the earth from the fire, the subtle from the gross, with great ingenuity. It rises from the earth to the sky and again descends into the earth, and receives the force of things superior and inferior. You shall have by this means the glory of the entire world. And therefore all obscurity shall flee from you. This is the strength strong of all strength. For it shall vanquish any thing subtle and shall penetrate any thing solid. Thus the world has been created.'

The fundamental key of the Great Work lies in the sexual union.

The formula of the Great Arcanum is the following:

'Inmissium membri virilis in vagina feminae sine ejaculatio seminis.'

Never to ejaculate the mercury of secret philosophy. To avoid the physiological orgasm. This is the fundamental key of the Great Work. The entity of semen is really and essentially the same mercury of secret philosophy which, when it is fertilized by the sulphur (living fire), becomes the master and regenerator of the salt (earthly man).

Only twelve thousand sealed of every one of the twelve tribes of Israel will be saved from the great cataclysm. (This number is symbolic).

Only those who have achieved the union of the cross-man with the triangle-spirit will be saved.

'After this I looked, and behold, a great multitude which no one could count, from every nation, from all tribes and peoples and tongues, standing before the throne and before the Lamb, clothed in white robes (Masters' robes), *with palm branches*

(of victory) *in their hands, and crying out with a loud voice, "Salvation belongs to our God who sits on the throne, and to the Lamb."* (Every man's inner Lamb). *And all the angels stood around the throne and around the elders and the four living creatures* (of the Great Arcanum), *and they fell down on their faces before the throne and worshipped God, saying, "Amen! Blessing and glory and wisdom and thanksgiving and honour and power and might be to our God for ever and ever! Amen." Then one of the elders addressed me, saying, "Who are these, clothed in white robes, and where have they come from?" I said to him, "Sir, you know." And he said to me, "These are those who have come out of the great tribulation; they have washed their robes and made them white in the blood of the Lamb* (who is within us all).*"'* (Rev. 7:9-14).

Only by working with the A.Z.F. Arcanum can we indeed incarnate him. We have to go down to the Forge of Vulcan (sex) to temper our sword and to attain Venusta Initiation.

Hercules goes down there to clean the inner stables of the soul with the sacred fire, and Perseus too, to cut the head of the ruler of this world with his flaming sword. Only in that way can we make our inner bodies white with the blood of our inner Lamb.

'For this reason they are before the throne of God, and serve him day and night in his temple, and the one who sits on the throne will shelter them with his presence.' (Rev. 7:15). The Father rejoices in the Son, and the Son rejoices in the Father. The Father is One with the Son, and the Son is One with the Father.

'They will hunger no more, and thirst no more. The sun will not strike them, nor any scorching heat. For the Lamb (their own inner Lamb) *who is in the middle of the throne will be their shepherd, and he will guide them to springs of living water. And God will wipe away every tear from their eyes.'* (Rev. 7: 16-17).

We have to resolve to die as egos in all the planes of cosmic consciousness. We have to admit our own misery and sin, so that our diamond soul can disappear into the Lamb.

The Inner Lord will shepherd us and will lead us to springs of waters of life. Those who drink of the springs of pure water of life will never be thirsty again, and rivers of pure water of life will flow from their interior.

We need to go through a true revolution of consciousness.

The experiences of life make the I complicated and stronger. We have been evolving for many millions of years now. So what? What have we gained from so many experiences? The simple man who lived eighteen million years ago is now the complicated and difficult, shrewd and selfish man of the big cities. Is this progress?

Let us look at a little child. How beautiful he is! How innocent he is! As the little child grows up little by little, as he evolves and begins gaining experiences through the different ages of life, he becomes more and more complicated, more and more shrewd, and when he reaches old age, he is full of spite, selfishness, distrust, resentment, evil things, etc. Is this evolution?

The experiences of life make the I complicated and stronger. We need to dissolve the I. When we have dissolved the I, there is then a total revolution of consciousness. The only thing for which the I is good is really for doing evil deeds. We need to go down to the Ninth Sphere (sex) to decapitate the I.

The I, evolving through the ages, grows stronger and stronger through experiences. We need no evolution now. What we need now is revolution.

When we dissolve the I, then the Inner Lamb will enter our soul.

When the Inner Lamb enters our soul, he is transformed into it. He is transformed into It, and It into Him.

From this divine and human symbiosis springs what we call the Son of Man.

That is the revolution of consciousness!

The four angels held back the four winds. They deferred the Karma that hangs over humanity, so that we could study the doctrine of the Adorable One.

Through the process of evolution we became tremendously destructive and wicked.

Now we need a total revolution of consciousness.

We need to decapitate and dissolve the I.

We need to incarnate the Immolated Lamb.

'And I heard the number of those who were sealed, one hundred and forty-four thousand sealed, from every tribe of the sons of Israel.' (Rev. 7:4).

CHAPTER 18

The Seventh Seal

*'A*nd *when the Lamb opened the seventh seal, there was si-lence in heaven for about half an hour.'* (Rev. 8:1).

The Adorable Saviour of the world confesses the sins of humanity before his Father and before the angels. The great orphan must be admitted to the hospital of angels.

The Divine Bridegroom wants to save his children. The adepts of the shadow want to take his little children with them, and He gathers them together under his loving arms, as the hen gathers her chicks together under her wings. A cancerous tumour has to be removed from the interior of the great orphan.

'And there was silence in heaven for about half an hour.' This scientific operation is inevitably very painful. There will be just a few survivors of the great catastrophe.

There will be a period of silence for about half an hour, a little fleeting time, but enough to secretly save the righteous.

The great apocalyptic events unfold on the shores of the immense sea of life.

'And I saw the seven angels (Gabriel, Raphael, Uriel, Michael, Samael, Zachariel and Oriphiel), *and seven trumpets were given to them.'* (Rev. 8:2).

'And another angel came and stood at the altar with a golden censer, and he was given a great deal of incense to mingle with the prayers of all the saints on the golden altar that is before the throne.' (Rev. 8:3).

91

'*And the smoke of the incense rose with the prayers of the saints before God from the hand of the angel.*' (Rev. 8:4). The saints will be cruelly persecuted by the atheists, and they will have to pray a great deal.

'*Then the angel took the censer and filled it with fire from the altar and threw it on the earth, and there were peals of thunder, voices, flashes of lightning and earthquakes.*' (Rev. 8:5).

Then the Gnostics will be persecuted to death. '*This gospel of the kingdom will be preached throughout the whole world as a testimony to all nations, and then the end will come.*' (Matthew 24:14). The materialistic atheists, the enemies of the Eternal, are full of false scientism. Atheists will persecute the Gnostics furiously. Atheists detest sexual magic. For that reason the Gnostics will be persecuted to death. Sex is the door to Eden, and the enemies of the Eternal do not want people to go in through that door. The Gnostics will multiply by their millions, but they will be cruelly persecuted and hated.

'*And the seven angels who had the seven trumpets made ready to blow them. And the first angel* (Gabriel) *blew his trumpet, and there followed hail and fire, mixed with blood, and they were hurled to the earth, and a third of the earth was burnt up, and a third of the trees were burnt up, and all green grass was burnt up.*' (Rev. 8:6-7).

The Philosophers' Stone is sex. The ancient wise men worshipped the sun under the symbolic form of a black stone. That is the Heliogabala Stone. Our Adorable Saviour taught us to build on the living rock. And the Adorable One said to Peter, '*Your name is Petrus, because you are the first stone on which I will build my church.*'

The Philosophers' Stone is the foundation of science, philosophy and religion.

The Philosophers' Stone is square as Saint John's Heavenly Jerusalem is. On one of its faces is the name of Adam, on another is the name of Eve, and then the names of Azoth and INRI on its two other sides.

The Philosophers' Stone is very sacred.

The science of the Antichrist has desecrated the sacred stone. Sanctuary unveiled, sanctuary desecrated. The precious stones of the temple are very sacred. Masters are children of the stones. No physician should touch the stones of the temple. Women patients should be seen by women doctors. But the times of the end have already come. And when the first angel blew his trumpet, there followed hail and fire, mixed with blood. Frozen water mixed with fire and blood — science, blood and passion. The temple of science was desecrated by the Antichrist, and the followers of Aesculapius committed fornication and adultery with the poor women patients. All green grass was burnt up. All honour was violated. The sacred Caduceus of Mercury fell on the pavement of the temple, smashed to pieces. The ears of science have grown ripe and now man will gather the poisonous fruit of desire by the sackful. The trumpet of the ruling angel of the moon has been blown.

'*And the second angel* (Raphael) *blew his trumpet, and something like a great mountain, burning with fire, was thrown into the sea* (the head of the whole of humanity), *and a third of the sea became blood.*' (Rev. 8:8). Millions of human beings will perish.

The karmic debts of each and every human being will be thoroughly checked before the great cataclysm. Exact mathematical calculations will be done before the great cataclysm.

Number is holy, infinite, eternal. Everything is directed by Holy Number. Once the accounts of the karmic books have been checked; once the mathematical calculations have been done, then the great cataclysm will come.

'*And a third of the living creatures in the sea died, and a third of the ships were destroyed.*' (Rev. 8:9). Millions of human beings will perish.

By 'a third' we understand the perfect triangle. The great catastrophe that is coming has a triple scope. It concerns the physical world, the soul world and the spiritual world. These three worlds correspond as a whole to the thirty-two paths of light, which are the sacred rungs of the Holy Ladder.

Raphael, the ruling angel of Mercury, has blown his trumpet, and mathematical calculations are being done in the internal temples of Karma.

The bodhisattva of Raphael is currently incarnated. Unfortunately he is now fallen. But that humble bodhisattva is currently struggling to rise.

'*And the third angel* (Uriel) *blew his trumpet, and a great star* (the star of bitterness) *fell from heaven, blazing like a torch, and it fell on a third of the rivers and on the fountains of water.*' (Rev. 8:10).

'*And the name of the star is Wormwood* (bitterness). *A third of the waters became wormwood, and many men died of the water, because it was made bitter.*' (Rev. 8:11).

The angel of Venus has blown his trumpet. Every event has a triple scope. The star of bitterness has a triple scope. The three worlds: the physical world, the world of the soul and the spiritual world, all correspond to the thirty-two paths of light, which are the rungs of the Holy Ladder.

Father, mother and child make a perfect ternary. Homes have been filled with bitterness. Ternary is fertility, generation, nature.

The waters are families and multitudes, peoples and tongues.

The waters became wormwood. The earth's homes were filled with fornication, hatred, adultery and great tribulation.

'*And the fourth angel* (Michael) *blew his trumpet, and a third of the sun was struck, and a third of the moon, and a third of the stars, so that a third of their light was darkened; a third of the day was kept from shining, and likewise a third of the night.*' (Rev. 8:12).

All cosmic events have a triple scope. The law of the triangle governs every cosmic manifestation.

The high zones of the earth's atmosphere will be completely altered by atomic explosions.

Then, by logical consequence, they will not be able to filter and analyze the rays of the sun, the moon and the stars.

Soon we will see the sun turning black as sackcloth and the moon becoming like blood. Then the stars will darken. There will be no light. An iron-reddish colour will cover the face of the earth.

All these great cosmic events have always a triple scope. The law of the triangle rules everything created.

With the complete alteration of the higher zones of the earth's atmosphere there will be terrible earthquakes and great seaquakes.

The sea will have a mysterious and strange sound. Terrible and monstrous waves will lash the shores. The cities, shaken by earthquakes, will become a pile of ruins.

Radioactivity will increase by the day, and great epidemics, unknown diseases, famines, misery and terrible tribulation will come with it. Crops will go to waste, and even the fishes of the sea will die.

'Woe to those who are with child and to those who give suck in those days! For there will be great distress on the earth and wrath on this people.' (Luke 21:23).

'And there will be signs in the sun, the moon and the stars, and on the earth distress of nations confused by the roaring of the sea and the waves, men fainting with fear and with foreboding of what is coming upon the world, for the powers of the heavens will be shaken.' (Luke 21:25-26).

'And I looked, and I heard an eagle crying with a loud voice as it flew in mid-heaven, "Woe, woe, woe to those who dwell on the earth, at the blasts of the other trumpets which the three angels are about to blow!"' (Rev. 8:13).

The ruler of this world, that I, that ego, that myself, who is within ourselves, thinks, with his fatal mind, of a comfortable

95

era of Aquarius, an era without problems of any kind, an era full of security. The ruler of this world is a real lord of comfort.

Woe to the dwellers of the earth! The Age of Aquarius is drawing near and the thunderbolt of Justice will fall on Babylon the Great, the mother of all fornication and abominations of the earth.

Aquarius influences the earth's atmosphere, and Peter, the Head of the Apostolic College, said, *'But the day of the Lord will come like a thief, and then the heavens will pass away with a loud noise, and the elements will be dissolved with fire, and the earth and the works that are on it will be burnt up.'* (2nd Peter 3:10).

Aquarius means the end to the Great Babylon. The times of the end have already come. The coming of the Christ means total revolution on the face of the earth.

The ancient earth was destroyed by water. This earth on which the Aryan race dwells will be destroyed by the fire of Aquarius.

The righteous must not fear. They will be secretly saved before the great cataclysm.

Lot, the righteous man, was taken out of Sodom when Sodom and Gomorrah were about to be destroyed by the terrifying fire of the earth's volcanoes. The righteous will be secretly evacuated from the Great Babylon.

The righteous will not pay for the sinners. This happened only once, and that time has passed.

CHAPTER 19

The Fifth Angel

*'A*nd the fifth angel* (Samael) *blew his trumpet, and I saw a star that had fallen from heaven to earth, and it was given the key to the shaft of the abyss.'* (Rev. 9:1).

Since the year 1950, a gigantic world is approaching our earth. That star has already fallen to our earth, and it was given the key to the shaft of the abyss.

We mean by this that the electromagnetic waves of that gigantic star have already touched the earth's axis.

That gigantic world was given the key to the shaft of the abyss.

The lower animal psychism of that gigantic planetary mass acts on the earth's humanity, sucking, absorbing, attracting all those billions of souls who do not have the sign of God on their foreheads.

That star acts from the depths of the abyss attracting billions of human beings. That star was given the key to the shaft of the abyss. Since the year 1950, billions of human souls are entering the abyss. Since 1950, the shaft of the abyss is opened.

The symbol of that star is the radiant cross. Once the sheep have been separated from the goats, the cross of the Redeemer will triumph.

This gigantic world will be visible to everyone in a few years. That star *'opened the shaft of the abyss, and from the shaft rose smoke like the smoke of a great furnace, and the sun and the air were darkened with the smoke from the shaft.'* (Rev. 9:2).

'And from the smoke came locusts on the earth, and they were given power like the power of scorpions of the earth. They were told not to harm the grass of the earth or any green growth or any tree, but only those of mankind who do not have the seal of God on their foreheads.' (Rev. 9:3-4).

Those locusts that come out of the smoke of the abyss are the human demons, the psychological I of every man.

The vultures of war, the magnates of gold and silver, the merchants of souls, bodies, perfumes and riches, the lords of politics, the great diplomats, the materialistic scientists, the lords of the atomic bomb and of the hydrogen bomb, etc. These human demons torment one another in the city and in the abyss, in their bodies or out of their bodies.

'And their torment was like the torment of a scorpion when it stings a man, and their torment lasts for five months.' (Rev. 9:5).

The number five is the number of rigour and of the Law, the number of Mars and of war. The two words 'five months' are symbolic.

We are now in the days of the great affliction. Woe to the dwellers of the earth! The times of the end have already come!

'And in those days (in these days, and in the abyss) *men will seek death and will not find it; they will long to die, and death will flee from them.'* (Rev. 9:6).

Life in the abyss is the same life that we have here in the physical plane, but millions of times more horrible, more material, darker, denser. In the abyss men are in their astral bodies, and they torment one another, and they long for death, and death flees from them.

The whole urban life transplanted to the abyss becomes millions of times coarser and terribly materialistic. Then men long for death, and death flees from them.

'In appearance the locusts were like horses ready for battle. On their heads were what looked like crowns of gold; their faces were like men's faces.' (Rev. 9:7).

This is the psychological I of every man. These are the vultures of war, the heads of state, the astute diplomats, the great generals.

'And their hair was like women's hair (full of feigned gentleness and hypocritical politeness), *and their teeth like lions' teeth; they had scales like iron breastplates, and the noise of their wings* (planes) *was like the noise of many chariots with horses rushing into battle. They have tails like scorpions, with stings* (powerful armies armed with stings, atomic bombs, remote-controlled rockets, hydrogen bombs, etc.), *and in their tails lies their power to harm men for five months.'* (Rev. 9:8-10). This is how the nations will pay for their karmic debts.

Those are the civil and military leaders of the world, the courteous diplomats, the great men of the earth. They have tails similar to those of scorpions, and in their tails are deadly and terrible stings.

These are the great military forces of the East and of the West, the military power of the earth, the great leaders, the great generals, the great diplomats, the powerful ones of the earth. That is this century!

'And they have as king over them the angel of the abyss; his name in Hebrew is Abaddon, and in Greek he is called Apollyon.' (Rev. 9:11).

'The first woe has passed. Behold, two woes are still to come.' (Rev. 9:12).

CHAPTER 20

The Sixth Trumpet

'*A*nd the sixth angel (Zachariel) *blew his trumpet, and I heard a voice from the four horns of the golden altar that was before God.*' (Rev. 9:13). The golden altar is man and woman, fire and water (IOD, HE, VAU, HE). The altar of God is nature.

'*Saying to the sixth angel who had the trumpet, "Release the four angels who are bound at the great river Euphrates."* (The four Devarajas who rule the four winds).' (Rev. 9:14).

'*And the four angels were released, who had been held ready for the hour, the day, the month and the year, to kill a third of mankind.*' (Rev. 9:15).

With the hydrogen bomb, the four angels at the earth's four cardinal points will be freed, who were designated for the day and the hour. Elements unknown to man will be released, and it will not be possible for human science to control them.

The hydrogen bomb will be the *pandemonium.*

'*And the number of the troops of cavalry was two hundred millions. I heard their number.*' (Rev. 9:16).

If the number two hundred millions is added up kabbalistically, we will have the Arcanum 2 of the Tarot: Woman, the woman pope, occult science.

Two is nature, and great nature will be terribly agitated by great cataclysms.

Atomic power and the hydrogen bomb will produce the frightful and terrible cataclysms of the times of the end. Nature's unknown elements will be released with the H-bomb, and no one will be able to control them. The human armies, armed with atomic potential, remote-controlled rockets, H-bombs, etc., will hurt great nature, and then, woe to the dwellers of the earth!

'And this was how I saw the horses in my vision; the riders wore breastplates the colour of fire and of sapphire and of sulphur, and the heads of the horses were like lions' heads, and fire and smoke and sulphur issued from their mouths.' (Rev. 9:17). These horses and these armies are peoples and multitudes and tongues. And fire of passion, smoke of laziness and sulphur of pain come out from the mouths of the dwellers of the earth.

Rajas and Tamas bring diseases and pain, darkness and despair, wars, famines, hospitals, etc. Rajas is emotion and passion. Tamas is inertia and laziness.

'By these three plagues a third of mankind was killed, by the fire and smoke and sulphur issuing from their mouths.' (Rev. 9:18). Woe to the dwellers of the earth! Woe to the scientists of the Antichrist! Woe to the vultures of war!

'For the power of the horses is in their mouths (speaking blasphemies) *and in their tails. Their tails are like serpents, with heads, and by means of them they wound.'* (Rev. 9:19). Those are the demons of the Great Babylon: men-demons.

'And the rest of mankind, who were not killed by these plagues, did not repent of the works of their hands or give up worshipping demons and idols of gold and silver and bronze and stone and wood, which cannot either see or hear or walk.' (Rev. 9:20).

'Nor did they repent of their murders or their sorceries or their fornication or their thefts.' (Rev. 9:21).

The times of the end have come, and we are in them. In the Arcanum 2,500 is contained the kabbalistic mystery of the times, of the day and of the hour.

CHAPTER 21

The Seventh Trumpet

'*And I saw another mighty angel coming down from heaven, wrapped in a cloud, with a rainbow over his head, and his face was like the sun, and his legs like pillars of fire.* (This angel is Oriphiel, the Genie of Saturn). *And he had a little scroll open in his hand. And he set his right foot on the sea, and his left foot on the land.*' (Rev. 10:1-2).

'*And he called out with a loud voice, like a lion roaring. When he called out, the seven thunders sounded.*' (Rev. 10:3). Those seven thunders are the sublime voices of the seven spirits before the throne, the seven powers of nature.

'*And when the seven thunders had sounded, I was about to write, but I heard a voice from heaven saying, "Seal up what the seven thunders have said, and do not write it down."*' (Rev. 10:4).

'*And the angel whom I saw standing on sea and land lifted up his right hand to heaven and swore by the one who lives for ever and ever, who created heaven and what is in it, the earth and what is in it, and the sea and what is in it, that they should be no more delay, but that in the days of the trumpet call to be sounded by the seventh angel, the mystery of God, as he announced to his servants the prophets, should be fulfilled.*' (Rev. 10:5-7).

Oriphiel, the Genie of Saturn, is the last one, and is the one who reaps the lives of men and of peoples with his sickle. '*Many are called and few are chosen.*' Those who will sit in victory at the Lord's table will be really very few. Dark humanity sank into the abyss.

'And the voice which I had heard from heaven spoke to me again, saying, "Go, take the scroll which is open in the hand of the angel who is standing on the sea and on the land." So I went to the angel and told him to give me the little scroll, and he said to me, "Take it and eat; it will be bitter to your stomach, but sweet as honey in your mouth."' (Rev. 10:8-9).

'And I took the little scroll from the hand of the angel and ate it; it was sweet as honey in my mouth, but when I had eaten it my stomach was made bitter. And I was told, "You must again prophesy about many peoples and nations and tongues and kings."' (Rev. 10:10-11).

In the days of the seventh angel, the kingdom of God will have been consummated as he announced to his servants the prophets. Let us see now what the Koran says:

'Heavenly revenge will come. No one will be able to stop it. The heavens will shake. The mountains will fall. On that day, unfortunate are those who have accused the apostles of imposture, those who spent their lives in frivolous disputes. "Throw yourselves into the live coals," they will be told. "Behold the fire, the reality of which you denied. You victims of the flames, whether you utter curses or you suffer in resignation, your lot will not change. You are getting now the just reward of your works.'

The Book of the Prophecy is indeed sweet in the mouth and bitter in the stomach.

On the day of the seventh angel the Jinas paradises, the lands of the fourth dimension in which divine humanity dwells, will be opened. That is the Garden of Delights. The righteous will live there.

'The chosen ones will be close to the Eternal. They will dwell in the Garden of Delights. A numerous company of old men and some youths will be happy guests there. They will rest on coaches adorned with gold and precious stones. They will look at each

other with affection. They will be served by children endowed with eternal youth. And they will pour exquisite wine into cups of different forms (the alchemist's wine of light). *Its vapour will not go up to their heads or will darken their reason. They will have the fruits that they wish at their disposal and the flesh of the rarest birds. The Huries with beautiful black eyes will be beside them. The whiteness of their faces will be like the shine of pearls. Their favours will be the reward to their virtue. Frivolous conversations will be banished from this mansion. In their hearts they will be no evil. Only the sweet name of peace will be heard there. How happy those who will stand at the right will be! They will walk among thornless lote trees and among artistically arranged banana trees. They will enjoy the thick foliage of them, being beside singing waters. There a multitude of diverse fruits will be offered to the hands wishing to take them. They will rest in elevated beds. Their wives will be a special creation — they will be virgins. They will love them and will enjoy the same youth as they do.* (Verses 11 to 36 of Chapter 56 of the Koran).

On the days of the seventh angel the Kingdom of God will be consummated, as he announced to his servants the prophets, and the Jinas paradises, in which divine humanity dwells, will be opened.

'The righteous will be the guests in the mansion of delights. They will gaze around as they lie in their nuptial beds. Joy will shine on their foreheads. They will drink an exquisite and sealed wine (the alchemist's wine of light). *The seal will be the musk. May those who wish the bliss strive to deserve it. This wine will be mixed with water from the Tasnim. A precious fountain in which those who are close to the Eternal will quench their thirst.* (Chapter 83, verses 22 to 28 of the Koran).

Musk, semen, is the origin and the seal of the great bliss. The alchemist's wine of light is mixed with water from the Tasnim. That pure water of life is the christonic semen.

The water must be transmuted into wine. That pure water of life must not be spilt. There can be sexual connection, but we must withdraw before the spasm in order to avoid seminal ejaculation. That is how we become gods and enter the Garden of Delights.

Semen is the precious fountain of life. *'A precious fountain in which those who are close to the Eternal will quench their thirst.'*

Mohammed rightly said indeed: *'The seal will be the musk. May those who wish the bliss strive to deserve it.'* This striving is only possible with sexual magic. That is the A.Z.F. Arcanum.

Those who want to enter the Garden of Delights must never ever spill their semen.

We must transmute desire into will, and withdraw from the sexual act before the spasm in order to avoid the ejaculation of the semen.

That is how we awaken the sacred fire and become gods. The semen must not leave our organism. The semen must never ever be spilt.

The sacred phallus can enter the womb, but the semen must not be spilt. This is the narrow and difficult door that leads us to the Light. This is the key to the awakening of Kundalini.

The A.Z.F. Arcanum is the stumbling block and the rock of scandal for the wicked. We went out of the Jinas paradises through the door of sex, and only through that door can we return to the Garden of Delights.

In the days of the seventh angel only those who have accepted the great A.Z.F. Arcanum will dwell in the Garden of Delights. That is the reason why Mohammed says the following:

'The true servants of God will enjoy happiness. They will have chosen food and exquisite fruits, and they will be served with honour. The gardens of voluptuousness will be their shelter. Full of mutual bliss, they will rest in their nuptial beds. They will be offered cups of clean, pure water having a delicious

taste (semen). *It will not confuse their faces, nor will it make them insensitive. Beside them there will be intact virgins, and they will humbly lower their eyes.* (Verses 39 to 47 of Chapter 37 of the Koran).

God really shines on the perfect couple.

Man and woman were born to love each other.

Blessed are the beings who know how to love each other!

CHAPTER 22

The Two Witnesses

'*And I was given a measuring rod like a staff* (the staff of Brahma, the rod of Aaron, symbol of the spinal cord and of its marvellous spinal canal. The flow of the creative energy of the Holy Spirit ascending along the spinal canal turns us into gods). *And I was told, "Rise and measure the temple of God and the altar and those who worship there.'* (Rev. 11:1).

The temple of God is man, and it has to be measured with a rod. If you want Initiation, write it on a rod.

'*"And do not measure the court outside the temple; leave that out, for it is given over to the nations, and they will trample over the holy city for forty-two months.'* (Rev. 11:2).

The court that is outside the temple is indeed the court of the profane, the court of fornicators. They will trample over the holy city for forty-two months. They desecrated the sacred city of the nine doors. The holy city is man, and the Ninth Sphere, or the ninth door, is sex. Fornicators have trampled over the holy city for forty-two months.

The science of numbers tells us that 4 + 2 = 6. Kabbalists know that the Arcanum 6 of the Tarot is *The Lover*. The number 666 (6 repeated three times) is the number of the great harlot.

'*"And I will grant my two witnesses power to prophesy for one thousand two hundred and sixty days, clothed in sackcloth."'* (Rev. 11:3).

This number is written in this way: 1,260. If we add up these numbers among themselves kabbalistically, we have the following result: 1 + 2 + 6 = 9. Nine is the Ninth Sphere. The Ninth Sphere is sex.

The great Master Hilarius IX says that in ancient times the descent to the Ninth Sphere was the greatest test for the supreme dignity of the Hierophant. Hermes, Buddha, Jesus Christ, Dante, Zoroaster, Mohammed, Rama, Krishna, Pythagoras, Plato and many others, had to go down to the Ninth Sphere to work with the fire and the water, origin of worlds, beasts, men and gods. Every genuine white initiation begins there.

The fire and the water ascend along the two sympathetic cords that coil around the spinal cord. In the East those two witnesses are called Ida and Pingala.

F + W = C. Fire plus water equals consciousness. The fire and the water produce the awakening of our cosmic consciousness. Then we prophesy for one thousand two hundred and sixty days, clothed in sackcloth, doing fast and penance.

The two sympathetic cords are the two witnesses along which the fire and the water of sex ascend. *'These are the two olive trees and the two lampstands which stand before the God of the earth* (the Inner God). *And if anyone would harm them, fire pours from their mouth and consumes their foes; if anyone would harm them, thus he is doomed to be killed.'* (Rev. 11:4-5).

The two witnesses produce the awakening of the Kundalini, then we receive the flaming sword that turns around threateningly as it guards the path to the Tree of Life.

It was necessary that the Lord should have died in that way. Now we must raise him up from the dead within ourselves. The two witnesses can kill and give life.

'They have power to shut the sky, so that no rain may fall during the days of their prophesying, and they have power over the waters to turn them into blood, and to smite the earth with every plague, as often as they desire.' (Rev. 11:6). If the sacred serpent goes up, it opens the sky. If it goes down, it shuts the

sky. The waters turn into blood when we fornicate, and the affliction of the abyss is more terrible than death.

Fornication is a sin against the Holy Spirit. Those who fornicate sin against their own bodies. Fornicating humanity is smitten with every plague.

All those who spill the semen are fornicators, even though they are officially married.

The two witnesses have the power to awaken the Kundalini (the pentecostal fire).

'And when they have finished their testimony, the beast that ascends from the abyss will make war on them and conquer them and kill them, and their dead bodies will lie in the streets of the great city which is spiritually called Sodom and Egypt, where their Lord was crucified.' (Rev. 11:7-8).

The prophets spoke in ancient times. The two witnesses gave their testimony then, and announced the times of the end. The two witnesses testified to the light, and the light came into the darkness, but the darkness did not know it.

The beast that ascended from the abyss — the Satan that is within us — made war on them and conquered them and killed them, because man gave himself over to fornication.

The bodies of the two witnesses were thrown into the street of Babylon the Great, the mother of all fornication and abominations of the earth, the land of Sodom and Egypt, where also their Lord was crucified — the valley of affliction where the great harlot lives.

'And for three days and a half men from the peoples and tribes and tongues and nations gaze at their dead bodies and refuse to let them be placed in a tomb.' (Rev. 11:9).

Jesus Christ, the Great Hierophant, said, *'I am able to destroy the temple of God, and to build it in three days.'* (Matthew 26:61). The body of the Saviour of the world remained three days in his Holy Sepulchre. Jonah was for three days in the belly of the whale.

The bodies of the two witnesses still do not deserve to descend to the holy sepulchre, because they are full of fornication. Man gave himself over to fornication and the two witnesses are dead.

'And those who dwell on the earth will rejoice over them and make merry and exchange presents, because these two prophets had been a torment to those who dwell on the earth.' (Rev. 11:10). The words of the prophets are a torment to those who dwell on the earth.

'And after the three and a half days a breath of life from God entered them, and they stood up on their feet, and great fear fell on those who saw them.' (Rev. 11:11).

The three days symbolize man's triune spirit: the Perfect Holy Trinity. The resurrection from the dead comes on the third day. We have suffered a great deal for three days, now the two witnesses will rise.

'And they heard a loud voice from heaven saying to them, "Come up here!" And in the sight of their foes they went up to heaven in a cloud.' (Rev. 11:12).

With the A.Z.F. Arcanum the two witnesses go up now. We are in the times of the end. This is the time when the prophecy is fulfilled. The resurrection of the two witnesses is an absolutely sexual problem.

When a man and a woman are able to withdraw from the sexual act without spilling the semen, the two witnesses rise, because the force of the Holy Spirit goes back inwards and upwards through them.

The two witnesses are the two marvellous sympathetic canals of the creative energy. The times of the end have already come.

The divulgence of the Great Arcanum, the resurrection of the two witnesses and the great final cataclysm accurately mark the end of the Aryan race.

112

Those human beings who do not accept scientific chastity will sink into the abyss. There will be a horrific cataclysm. However, no human being can know the date, or the day, or the hour. A planetary crash, a collision of worlds will come, and only those who have raised their two witnesses from the dead will be saved.

'And at that hour there was a great earthquake, and a tenth of the city fell; seven thousand people were killed in the earthquake, and the rest were terrified and gave glory to the God of heaven.' (Rev. 11:13).

A tenth of the Great Babylon will fall. The wheel of destiny will turn and the great harlot will sink into the abyss.

The number 10 is the Wheel of Destiny, the Arcanum 10 of the Tarot.

Seven thousand people were killed in the earthquake. The Arcanum 7 means expiation, Karma, punishment. The great harlot will die indeed, together with those of the peoples and tribes and tongues that are so numerous as the grains of sand in the sea.

The two witnesses will speak before the great cataclysm that is drawing near. Before the horrific catastrophe that is coming, the heavens will unfold with a loud noise and the human multitudes of Mars, Mercury, Venus and of other worlds will come to the earth in their spaceships. The brother humanities of other planets will come to teach us law and order. We will be given the opportunity to listen to the Son of Man.

Then... Woe to those who repudiate the Son of Man! Woe to those who reject the Great Arcanum! Woe to those who keep spilling the semen!

The man of the earth has embarked on the conquest of space, and will soon knock with his spaceships on the doors of other inhabited worlds. The result of his forwardness will be the response of the Son of Man: *'Then he will come on the clouds of heaven and every eye will see him.'*

The Son of Man represents the Divine Humanity. The Son of Man represents the superior multitudes in other inhabited worlds.

Every cosmic rocket launched into space gets us closer to the great cosmic event. Woe to those who do not accept the last word of the Son of Man! The great cataclysm will come after that!

'The second woe has passed. Behold, the third woe is soon to come.' (Rev. 11:14).

'And the seventh angel blew his trumpet, and there were loud voices in heaven, saying, "The kingdom of the world has become the kingdom of our Lord and of his Christ, and he will reign for ever and ever."' (Rev. 11:15).

'And the twenty-four elders who sit on their thrones before God fell on their faces and worshipped God, saying, "We give thanks to you, Lord God Almighty, who are and who were, for you have taken your great power and begun to reign.' (Rev. 11:16-17).

'"And the nations raged, but your wrath has come, and the time for the dead to be judged, for rewarding your servants, the prophets and saints, and those who fear your name, both small and great, and for destroying the destroyers of the earth (the vultures of war and the scientists of the Antichrist)."' (Rev. 11:18).

The Last Judgement was already done on 12th April, 1950. The gods judged the great harlot and deemed her unworthy. The sentence of the gods was: To the Abyss! To the Abyss! To the Abyss! The earth will go through a process of planetary disintegration and reintegration. No one but the Father knows the day or the hour.

'And the temple of God in heaven was opened, and the ark of his covenant was seen within his temple. And there were flashes of lightening, voices, peals of thunder, earthquakes, and heavy hail.' (Rev. 11:19).

114

The Ark of the Covenant is sex. The Ark of the Covenant is the Ark of Science. The Ark of the Testimony is the Ark of the Covenant. Within the Ark of the Covenant is the rod of Aaron, symbol of the phallus, and the vessel, or gomor, full of manna, symbol of the womb. (See Exodus 16:31-36).

In the union of the phallus and the womb lies the key to all power. Within the Ark of Science are the Tables of the Law.

All those who violate the divine Decalogue will sink into the abyss. Only in the Ark of the Covenant will we attain the miracle of our salvation.

CHAPTER 23

The Woman and the Dragon

'*And a great portent appeared in heaven, a women clothed with the sun, with the moon under her feet, and on her head a crown of twelve stars. She was pregnant and she cried out in her birth pangs, in anguish for delivery.*' (Rev. 12:1-2).

With this great portent that appeared in the heaven of the end of times, we the Brothers teach man how to build the temple.

The temple has to be built on the living rock, but the rock is full of prickly pears, with sharp spines that hurt the flesh.

The Son of Man is always born from the womb of a virgin.

When our adorable Saviour was bleeding on his cross, he taught us the secret of the woman clothed with the sun and of the Venusta Initiation.

'*And when Jesus saw his mother, and the disciple whom he loved standing near, he said to his mother, "Woman, behold your son!"*' (John 19:26).

'*Then he said to the disciple, "Behold your mother!" And from that hour the disciple took her to his own home.*' (John 19:27).

The name of this disciple was John. This name is broken down into the five vowels: I, E, O, U, A, N. John is the Word. John is the Son, and he is always born from the womb of a woman.

We mean by this that only by practising sexual magic can we incarnate the Christ within ourselves.

Only by working with the A.Z.F. Arcanum do we attain Venusta Initiation. The Word is always born of Immaculate Conceptions. The Son of Man is always a child of a Virgin-Mother.

That woman, clothed with the sun and crowned with twelve stars and with the moon under her feet, is the woman who has succeeded in achieving the secret degree of Virgin-Mother. She is Urania-Venus, the Queen of Heaven, who, being pregnant, is having labour pains.

'And another portent appeared in heaven; behold, a great red dragon, with seven heads and ten horns, and seven diadems on his heads.' (Rev. 12:3).

That dark dragon revolves with the wheel of the ages. That dragon of darkness came up from the abyss, and when the wheel revolves again, he will fall back into the abyss.

The dragon of the abyss is the evil of the world. He is the Black Lodge. He is the secret enemy with his terrible evil deeds.

With the number seven we will expiate our errors. The ten horns symbolize the wheel of destiny. The wheel will revolve, and the beast will sink into the abyss. The times of the end have already come, and no one knows exactly for how long these times of the end will last.

The dragon of darkness is the ruler of this world.

The dragon of darkness is the I, the myself, the ego that is within us (Satan).

'And his tail swept down a third of the stars of heaven and threw them to the earth. And the dragon stood before the woman who was about to bear a child, so that he might devour her child as soon as it was born.' (Rev. 12:4).

Thousands of bodhisattvas really fell during the iron age. The dragon of darkness stands before the woman to devour her child. The secret enemy wants to devour us.

Nirvana has periods of activity and periods of deep rest.

Since 19th February 1919, Nirvana came into activity, because the times of the end have already come and we need help. On 19th February at 4 p.m. the Virgins began to be born. Millions of virgins of Nirvana are now reincarnating to help us.

It is astonishing to see those virgins now reincarnated as poor women, as humble maids.

That is the great portent that appeared in heaven. She is Venus-Urania. She is the woman clothed with the sun and with the moon under her feet.

She was born to be a virgin mother. The degree of virgin is the Buddhic state.

The virgin mother, being pregnant, is in anguish for delivery, and the dragon of darkness wants to devour her child and to thwart in us the incarnation of the Christ.

The Antichrist hates the A.Z.F. Arcanum, and does not want the Christ to be born in us. *'Many are called and few are chosen.'*

On the long winter nights the Christ is born in the heart of man. On nights of sorrow and darkness and tears the Saviour is born in the manger of the world.

'And she gave birth to a son, one who is to rule all the nations with a rod of iron, but her child was caught up to God and to his throne.' (Rev. 12:5).

That woman, clothed with the sun and crowned with twelve stars and with the moon under her feet, always gives birth to a male child, the Son of Man, who is very strong in these times of the end, and he must rule the nations with a rod of iron. The Son of Man is really caught up to God and to his throne.

'And the woman fled into the wilderness, where she has a place prepared by God so that there she can be nourished for one thousand two hundred and sixty days.' (Rev. 12:6).

Every virgin mother lives in her own wilderness away from the world, the demon and the flesh. While the virgin mothers live in the world, they create their own wilderness for themselves.

The kabbalistic number 1,260 is broken down in this way: $1 + 2 + 6 = 9$. Nine is indeed the Ninth Sphere (sex). The Son of Man is born amidst the fire and the water of the Ninth Sphere. Every woman who has attained the esoteric degree of Virgin is kept there for one thousand two hundred and sixty days.

'And war broke out in heaven; Michael and his angels fought against the dragon, and the dragon and his angels fought back.' (Rev. 12:7).

And Michael and all of us, the Brothers of the Ray of Strength, fought against the dragon of darkness and against the dark legions of the Black Lodge. This fight against the dragon and his black angels began exactly in the year 1950.

'But they were defeated and there was no longer any place for them in heaven.' (Rev. 12:8). The battles between the legions of light and of darkness have been terrible and frightful in the inner worlds.

'And the great dragon was thrown down, that ancient serpent, who is called the Devil and Satan, the deceiver of the whole world — he was thrown down to the earth, and his angels were thrown down with him.' (Rev. 12:9).

The great Black Lodge and all the 'left-handed' adepts dwelt usually in the different atomic regions of nature. Since the year 1950, the great battle between the White Lodge and the Black Lodge began.

Since the year 1950, the followers of Lucifer and Ahriman, the followers of Bons and Dugpas, the enemies of the Fourth Path, the Nicolaitans and the tantric Anagarikas are all entering the abyss.

The abyss is indeed the Avitchi of the Hindustanis. The abyss is the Kliphos of the Kabbalah. Those Kliphos are atomic, dark, sublunar.

The antithesis of those Kliphos is a superdivine atom that is related to the Church of Laodicea or the one-thousand-petalled lotus.

Ultimately, we are that superdivine atom. The name of that atom is Ain Soph.

The Ain Soph is our atomic star. That star shines full of glory in the Absolute Abstract Space.

Kether, Chokmah and Binah emanate from that star. The Father, the Son and the Holy Spirit of every man emanate from that star.

The abyss is the antithesis of Ain Soph, the fatal shadow of Ain Soph.

Ain Soph is omniscience and happiness. The adepts of the shadow of the lunar path dwell in the abyss.

'And I heard a loud voice in heaven, saying, "Now the salvation and the power and the kingdom of our God and the authority of his Christ has come, for the accuser of our brothers has been thrown down, who accuses them day and night before our God.' (Rev. 12:10). The accuser of our brothers is the black dragon. The accuser of our brothers stoned to death, poisoned and crucified the prophets. The accuser of our brothers is the Black Lodge.

Now the saints of the Lord will come out in victory. They have defeated Satan.

'"And they have conquered him by the blood of the Lamb and by the word of their testimony, for they did not love their lives even until death.' (Rev. 12:11).

'Rejoice then, O heavens and you who dwell in them! But woe to you, O earth and sea, for the devil has come down to you in great wrath, because he knows that his time is short!"' (Rev. 12:12). The Satan, being in great wrath and knowing that his time is short, will precipitate the atomic war. In this century there will be many wars to death and frightful cataclysms.

'And when the dragon saw that he had been thrown down to the earth (and to the abyss), *he pursued the woman who had given birth to the male child.'* (Rev. 12:13).

*'And the woman was given the two wings of the great eagle
so that she might fly from the serpent into the wilderness, to the
place where she is to be nourished for a time, and times, and
half a time.'* (Rev. 12:14).

In these times of the end the nirvanic women will withdraw
to the wilderness of their own lives, fleeing from the tempting
serpent. Many become nuns for a while. Most of them are
household maids. In this way they earn their daily bread. That
is how they serve with humility. They have the wings of the eagle of the spirit, and take shelter in the wilderness. Those virgin
mothers indeed suffer a great deal. To them, life in the world is
a wilderness. They complain about the time wasted. In this terrible wilderness they cannot find a man who wants to become
christified.

There they are nourished for a time and times and half a time.
Matters related to profession, job matters. A time: the job rou-
tine. Times: moving homes, changing offices, new jobs. Half a
time: when the hour strikes, when the man who they are waiting for appears in the wilderness of life.

*'And the serpent poured water like a river out of his mouth
after the woman, to sweep her away with the flood. But the earth
came to the help of the woman, and the earth opened its mouth
and swallowed the river which the dragon had poured from his
mouth.'* (Rev. 12:15-16).

The tempting serpent of Eden tempts the woman clothed with
the sun, and tries to make her fall sexually, but those virgin
mothers transmute their creative energies and fly high in the
wings of the spirit.

The philosophical earth, that is, the physical organism, swal-
lows the river; it transmutes it into light and fire. That river is
the universal dissolvent of Alchemy: the *lapis philosophorum*,
the pure gold or *summa materia*. It is also called *menstruum uni-
versalis*. That is the essence which the dragon pours out of his
mouth and which we must transmute to fly in the wings of the
spirit as eagles of light.

That is how Urania-Venus defends herself against the tempting serpent that made Eve-Venus sin.

There are several kinds of women. Let us see:

1. Eve-Venus. The animal-like, instinctive, brutal woman.

2. Venus-Eve. The very human woman who loves when she finds a sexually passionate man who loves her.

3. Venus-Urania. The very human and conscious woman, full of both a deep spiritual feeling and a human feeling.

4. Urania-Venus. The mother of the Son of Man, the virgins of Nirvana, the woman clothed with the sun and with the moon under her feet. That woman is crowned with twelve stars symbolizing the seven churches and the five senses, that is, the twelve faculties.

Only woman can establish justice on the face of the earth, because she has the power to awaken man's flaming fire. The key lies in the A.Z.F. Arcanum.

She gives man the sword. She is Urania-Venus with the sword in her hand. She stands before the cosmic scales in the Arcanum 8.

She is the mother of the Son of Man. She wants to crush the head of the tempting serpent to tame it and raise it along the spinal canal.

Unfortunately, as Goethe said, *'Law of the sad and grave man, he searches, struggles, becomes agitated. What he needs most is what he knows least.'*

Man needs the A.Z.F. Arcanum, and he does not know it. That is what he needs most and what he knows least.

We the Brothers of the Temple are now teaching it, but the dwellers of the earth hate it.

The dragon tempts Urania-Venus, and comes out defeated.

'Then the dragon was angry with the woman, and went off to make war on the rest of her offspring, on those who keep the commandments of God and bear testimony to Jesus Christ.' (Rev. 12:17).

CHAPTER 24

The Two Beasts

'*And I stood on the sand of the sea, and I saw a beast rising out of the sea, with ten horns and seven heads, with ten diadems on its horns and a blasphemous name on its heads.*' (Rev. 13:1).

That beast with seven heads represents fornicating humanity. The ten horns symbolize the wheel of destiny. The beast rises out of the abyss and falls back into the abyss. The ten diadems on its seven heads mean that the beast reigns supreme during the Iron Age or Kali Yuga. However, when the wheel of destiny turns on its axis, the beast will tumble down into the precipice.

'*And the beast that I saw was like a leopard, its feet were like a bear's, and its mouth was like a lion's mouth. And to it the dragon gave his power and his throne and great authority. One of its heads seemed to have a mortal wound, but its mortal wound was healed, and the whole earth followed the beast with wonder.*' (Rev. 13:2-3).

When the Brothers of the Temple examine the head of the wounded and healed beast, they see a new symbol. They see a man like a gorilla in appearance, full of evil intelligence. The gorilla-man, frightful and terrible, conducts four beasts ahead of himself, he being the fifth. The four beasts are walking in chains and he is leading them. By this symbol we understand that the wounded head is the wicked man of the fifth race, the present-day man. This evil race throws itself into a fratricidal and barbaric war, and after being mortally wounded, it is healed and the whole earth follows the beast with wonder. The inner

125

bodies are indeed also wounded in the battle. However, they are healed with the help of the masters of medicine.

'*And they worshipped the dragon* (the Satan), *for he had given his authority to the beast, and they worshipped the beast, saying, "Who is like the beast, and who can fight against it?"'* (Rev. 13:4). Everyone thinks that they are civilized, and they are worshipping the great beast. Everyone is worshipping the I, the myself, the Satan that is within us. People live in evil. Everyone loves the beast, and wallows in mud.

'*And the beast was given a mouth uttering haughty and blasphemous words, and it was allowed to exercise authority for forty-two months.*' (Rev. 13:5). The beast has preeminence during the whole Kali Yuga and reigns supreme. The beast is the great harlot whose reign is over.

'*And it opened its mouth to utter blasphemies against God, blaspheming his name* (with atheism) *and his dwelling* (fornication), *and those who dwell in heaven* (the saints).' (Rev. 13:6).

'*And it was allowed to make war on the saints and to conquer them* (many initiates fell). *And authority was given to it over every tribe and people and tongue and nation.*' (Rev. 13:7) The whole of humanity capitulated to the great beast that rises out of the abyss and is now falling back into the abyss.

'*And all who dwell on the earth will worship it, everyone whose name has not been written from the foundation of the world in the book of life of the Lamb that was killed.*' (Rev. 13:8).

The Book of Life is called *Aliin* in the Koran, and it contains the behaviour of the righteous and of the angels.

The book of the lost ones is called among the Mohammedans by the name of *Syyin*. The good and bad works are weighed in the scales of Cosmic Justice.

Those who are not written in the Book of Life are now sinking into the frightful abyss. The Gnostic faith is the only faith that can save the lost ones. The Lamb was killed from the foundation of the world, when we began to fornicate. Now we must raise the Lamb up within ourselves with the A.Z.F. Arcanum. That is sexual magic.

'If anyone has an ear, let him hear. If anyone takes to captivity, to captivity he goes; if anyone kills with the sword, with the sword must he be killed. Here is a call for the endurance and faith of the saints.' (Rev. 13:9-10).

Law is law. One has to face the consequences of one's actions. The saints know the law and for that reason they are patient. Truly, truly I say to you: The times of the end have already come. If anyone takes to captivity, to captivity he goes. He who lives by the sword, dies by the sword. Only by entering the Ark of Science can we be saved. We went out of Eden through the door of sex. Only through that door can we enter Eden. Eden is sex itself.

No one can enter Eden through false doors. Law is law. We have to go in through the same door we went out. That is the law.

The Opus Magnus is the science of sexual transmutation. We must bring back the energy of the Third Logos inwards and upwards. That is how we become gods. Water and oil are needed in the alchemist's Great Work — half water and half oil. Those who despise the water fail in the Great Work. We can become enlightened only with our own spiritual oil, when we have pure water of life (accumulated semen).

'What are the these two branches of the olive trees, which are beside the two golden pipes from which the oil is poured out?' 'These are the two children of oil who stand before the Lord of the whole earth'. (See Zechariah 4:12-14).

These are the two witnesses that ultimately spring from the lake. They come out of the seminal vesicles. The transmuted sexual energy, the oil of pure gold, flows through those two olive trees. Those who affirm that there are many paths to reach God and that sex is just one of many, are really despising the pure water of life, and consequently they fail and will sink into the abyss.

Truly, truly I say to you that throughout eternity only one, and absolutely one narrow door, and only one narrow and difficult path that leads to the light have been known. Sex is that door and that path.

'Strive to enter through the narrow door (sex), *for many, I tell you, will seek to enter and will not be able.'* (Luke 13:24). The door is narrow and the path that leads to the Light is also narrow, and those who find it are very few. Our Adorable Saviour Jesus Christ never said that there are many paths. He spoke clearly and plainly only about one door and about one path (sex). (See John 10:7-9,14).

We the Brothers of the Temple invite you, dear reader, to study the four gospels. There you can see for yourself that there is only one door and only one narrow and difficult path.

Those preachers who affirm the existence of many paths to reach God are ignorant of the fact that in the Great Work we need half oil and half water.

'Then I saw another beast that rose out of the earth; it had two horns like a lamb and it spoke like a dragon. It exercises all the authority of the first beast in its presence, and makes the earth and its inhabitants worship the first beast, whose mortal wound was healed.' (Rev. 13:11-12).

'And it performs great signs, even making fire come down from heaven to earth in the sight of men; and by the signs which it is allowed to perform in the presence of the beast, it deceives those who dwell on the earth, telling them to make an image for the beast which was wounded by the sword and yet lived.' (Rev. 13:13-14).

This beast that has two horns like a lamb and speaks like a dragon is the materialistic science of the dwellers of the earth. The great beast is indeed double, because it has a mind that speaks haughty words. Materialistic science plays with what it does not know, and limps about in the dark.

128

Materialistic science deceives those who dwell on the earth by the signs which it is allowed to perform in the presence of the beast: remote-controlled rockets, cosmic rockets, radio-television, ultramodern planes, hydrogen bombs that make fire come down from heaven on defenceless cities, atomic bombs, atomic submarines, deadly rays, etc.

All those inventions are the signs with which the two-horned beast deceives those who dwell on the earth. Then men, being deceived, worship the great beast, and say, 'There is no one like the beast! Who can be superior to the beast!'

'*And it was allowed to give breath to the image of the beast so that the image of the beast could even speak, and to cause those who would not worship the image of the beast to be killed.*' (Rev. 13:15). The men of materialistic science poison the multitudes with their theories. Then the image of the beast speaks. The saints who refuse to worship the beast are killed, persecuted, imprisoned and hated. The two-horned beast is terrible.

'*And it causes all, both small and great, both rich and poor, both free and slave, to be marked on the right hand or on the forehead, so that no one can buy or sell unless he has the mark, that is, the name of the beast or the number of its name.*' (Rev. 13:16-17).

'*This calls for wisdom: let him who has understanding reckon the number of the beast, for it is the number of man. Its number is six hundred and sixty-six.*' (Rev. 13:18).

The mark of the beast is the two horns on the forehead. Millions and millions of human beings already have the mark of the beast on their foreheads and on their hands. Almost all the human population of this valley of tears already has the mark of the beast on their foreheads and on their hands. All those souls are lost, and since 1950 they are entering the abyss. Human evolution failed completely.

The world is indeed so lost that in the world of commerce no one can buy or sell unless they have the mark of the beast on their foreheads and on their hands. Such is the world of business.

The number of the great beast is six hundred and sixty-six. That is the number of man because that number is kabbalistically broken down in this way: $6 + 6 + 6 = 18$. Then, if we add up every figure in this number, we have the following: $1 + 8 = 9$. Nine is sex. Nine is man, because man is a child of sex.

To sum up, the Arcana 18 and 9 are contained in the number 666. The Arcanum 18 represents the abyss, darkness — the sexual temptations against which the initiate has to fight.

The Arcanum 9 is the Ninth Sphere, Initiation.

The gods judged the great harlot, whose number is 666.

The sentence of the gods was: To the abyss! To the abyss! To the abyss!

CHAPTER 25

The Lamb in Zion

'*And I looked, and behold, the Lamb stood on Mount Zion, and with him a hundred forty-four thousand who had his name and his Father's name written on their foreheads.*' (Rev. 14:1). Mount Zion is the higher worlds.

The number one hundred forty-four thousand, the number of those who have his Father's name written on their foreheads, is a symbolic and kabbalistic number. 144,000 is broken down in this way: 1 + 4 + 4 = 9. This number 9 is the Ninth Sphere, sex.

Only by practising the Great Arcanum can we be saved and receive our Father's name on our foreheads. The people of Zion is the people of Israel (God's spiritual people). This people is made up of all who practise sexual magic (people of chastity).

'*And I heard a voice from heaven like a sound of many waters* (the seminal waters), *and like the sound of loud thunder; the voice I heard was like the sound of harpers playing on their harps.*' (Rev. 14:2).

'*And they sing a new song before the throne and before the four living creatures* (of Alchemy) *and before the elders. No one could learn that song except the hundred and forty-four thousand who had been redeemed from the earth* (with great sacrifice).' (Rev. 14:3).

'*It is these who have not defiled themselves with women, for they are virgins* (it is these who have learned to restrain the beast in order not to ejaculate the semen). *It is these who follow the Lamb wherever he goes. These have been redeemed from mankind as first fruits for God and the Lamb.'* (Rev. 14:4).

'And in their mouths no lie was found, for they are spotless.' (Rev. 14:5).

'And I saw another angel flying in mid-heaven, with an eternal gospel to proclaim to those who dwell on the earth, to every nation and tribe and tongue and people. And he said with a loud voice, "Fear God and give him glory, for the hour of his judgement has come; and worship him who made heaven and earth, the sea and the fountains of water."' (Rev. 14:6-7).

'And another angel, a second, followed, saying, "Fallen, fallen is Babylon the great! (Babylon the great, the mother of all fornication and abominations of the earth: Paris, Rome, London, Berlin, United States, etc. — the present civilization). *She has made all nations drink of the wine of the wrath of her fornication."'* (Rev. 14:8).

'And another angel, a third, followed them, saying with a loud voice, "If anyone worships the beast and its image, and receives a mark on his forehead or on his hand, he also will drink the wine of the wrath of God, poured unmixed into the cup of his anger, and he will be tormented with fire and sulphur in the presence of the holy angels and in the presence of the Lamb.' (Rev. 14:9-10).

All those who worship the beast of passions and its image (intellectualism devoid of spirituality) will burn in the abyss amid the fire and sulphur of their own desires.

It is preferable to pay the whole Karma here, in the physical plane, and never in the inner worlds. Nemesis, Karma, however grave it may be in the physical plane, is very sweet compared to the Karma in the astral plane and in the abyss.

'"And the smoke of their torment goes up for ever and ever. There is no rest day or night for those who worship the beast and its image and for anyone who receives the mark of its name."' (Rev. 14:11).

The intellect put absolutely in the service of the Spirit is a very precious instrument for the Great Work of the Father. A mystic without intellect fails through lack of culture. The intellect put in the service of the beast is satanic. From intellectualism without spirituality arise rogues. Rogues are exactly the image of the beast.

In the abyss the adepts of the shadow torment each other with their hatred, intrigues, slander, anger, greediness, lust, etc., and the smoke of their torment goes up for ever and ever. The saints know this, and for that reason they are patient.

'Here is a call for the endurance of the saints, those who keep the commandments of God and the faith of Jesus.' (Rev. 14:12).

'And I heard a voice from heaven saying, "Write this: Blessed are the dead who from now on die in the Lord." "Yes," says the Spirit, "they will rest from their labours, for their deeds follow them."' (Rev. 14:13).

When a man dies, something continues. That something is his thought. All his desires, all his thoughts of desire continue, and that has been already proven. The total sum of all our mental values continues. The total sum of all those values of desire constitute the I, the myself, the ego, our individuality. The I reincarnates to satisfy its desires.

Blessed are those who die in the Lord; they will enter Nirvana forever. All those who decapitate and dissolve the I die while still alive; they die in the Lord. Where the I is, there cannot be truth. The Lord is Truth. Lord Buddha taught us an essence, a law and an end.

The essence is the *ens seminis*. The law is the A.Z.F. Arcanum. The end is Nirvana. Thus said the Buddha:

'If you understand, O Kasyapa, that all beings are made of one and the same essence (the ens seminis), *and that there is only one truth* (the Christ), *and you live in accordance with this understanding, you will attain Nirvana.*

'*Tathagata gives joy to the whole world, like a cloud that pours its waters* (the semen) *on both righteous men and sinners* (everyone has it). *He shows the same compassionate feelings both for the great and for the small, both for the wise and for the ignorant, both for the virtuous and for sinners.*

'*He makes the vast cloud laden with water pour its water in the form of rain upon meadows and bramble patches, mountains and valleys, orchards and fields. And all drink the rain water* (semen), *which is one and the same essence; and trees, plants and herbs grow and blossom and bear fruit, each according to its own species and nature. Taking root in the same soil, all the plants in a field or in an orchard receive the same water* (semen), *which gives life to them all.*

'*Tathagata knows, O Kasyapa!, the law whose virtue is knowledge and whose end is the peace of Nirvana* (the law of the A.Z.F. Arcanum).

'*He is the one and the same for everyone, but he does not manifest himself to everyone in the same manner, but to everyone according to their needs. He does not give everyone the fullness of knowledge from the beginning, but he takes everyone's predisposition into account.*' In the past the A.Z.F. Arcanum was secretly told only to initiates. The Buddha taught the key of the A.Z.F. Arcanum to those of his disciples who were well prepared.

Whoever wants to die in the Lord must wash his feet in the waters of renunciation. Lord Buddha taught chastity as the basic foundation of Initiation.

Buddha asked his disciples the following question: '*Tell me, O disciples!, when does a disciple stop being a disciple?*' And Sariputra answered, '*The good disciple must not break chastity. He who breaks it is no longer a disciple of Sakya Muni.*' These are quoted words of the Gospel of Lord Buddha, transcribed from the Pitakas or Holy Scriptures of Buddhism. See the text by Yogi Kharishnanda.

Master Huiracocha gave the Supreme Key of Chastity in Latin. Let us see it: *'Immissio membri virilis in vagina feminae sine ejaculatio seminis.'*

Whoever wants to die in the Lord must practise the Ten Commandments of the New Era:

1. You shall love your Inner God and your neighbour as yourself.
2. You shall study the Secret Doctrine of the Saviour of the world.
3. Never vituperate against your neighbour, or speak immodest o vain words.
4. You shall sacrifice yourself for the sake of humanity, and love your worst enemies.
5. You must obey the will of the Father, in heaven as it is on earth.
6. You shall not commit fornication or adultery in thought, word or deed.
7. You shall fight against the world, the demon and the flesh.
8. You shall be infinitely patient and merciful.
9. You shall practise the A.Z.F. Arcanum with your wife.
10. You shall wash your feet in the waters of renunciation.

By practising these Ten Commandments you will die in the Lord.

'Then I looked, and behold, a white cloud, and seated on the cloud was one like the Son of Man, with a golden crown on his head, and a sharp sickle in his hand.' (Rev. 14:14).

'And another angel came out of the temple, calling with a loud voice to the one who sat on the cloud, "Put in your sickle, and reap, for the hour to reap has come, for the harvest of the earth is fully ripe.' (Rev. 14:15). The hour has come.

'And the one who sat on the cloud swung his sickle on the earth, and the earth was reaped.' (Rev. 14:16). The hour to reap has come.

'And another angel came out of the temple in heaven, and he too had a sharp sickle. Then another angel came out from the altar, the angel who has power over fire, and he called with a loud voice to the one who had the sharp sickle, "Put in your sickle, and gather the clusters of the vine of the earth, for its grapes are ripe."' (Rev. 14: 17-18).

The power of fire lies in sex. Angels and devils, gods and beasts, all come out of sex. Man is the priest; woman is the altar.

One sows in sex and one reaps in sex. If the crop is good; it is a crop of gods. When the crop is bad; it goes to waste in the abyss. The North American wise kabbalist Manly H. Hall, mentioned by the great Master of the White Lodge Dr Francisco A. Propato, says in his book on Man's Occult Anatomy the following: *'Those who are unable to raise the fire of the spinal cord along the sushumna canal will be thrown into a side kingdom, similar to that of the present-day simians* (apes or monkeys).*'*

'And the angel swung his sickle on the earth and gathered the vintage of the earth, and threw it into the great wine press of the wrath of God.' This Verse 19 of Chapter 14 of the Book of Revelation is definitive.

The angel threw the whole vintage into the great wine press of the wrath of God. The Great White Lodge knows that human evolution on earth is lost. Human evolution failed completely and humanity sank into the abyss.

'And the wine press was trodden outside the city, and blood flowed from the wine press, as high as a horse's bridle, for one thousand six hundred stadia.' (Rev. 14: 20).

This kabbalistic number is broken down in this way: 1 + 6 = 7.

The human race will expiate all its evil deeds with supreme pain. The three ineffable beings of this Chapter 14 of the Book of Revelation correspond to the three aspects of humanity: world, family and man. The three angels of the Most High punish nation, family and man.

Law is law, and the law is fulfilled. The three obey the Son of Man.

The Lord of all Power sits on a cloud of glory.

The Lord of all Perfection wears a golden crown on his head and holds a sharp sickle in his hand.

CHAPTER 26

THE SEVEN ANGELS AND
THE SEVEN BOWLS

'*And I saw another portent in heaven, great and wonderful, seven angels with seven plagues, which are the last, for with them the wrath of God is ended.*' (Rev. 15:1).

The seven angels are: Gabriel, Raphael, Uriel, Michael, Samael, Zachariel and Oriphiel. Of all the seven, the fifth angel is the one who has suffered most. All of them carry out superior orders and act in accordance with the Law. After the Atlantean catastrophe the bodhisattva of the fifth fell, and after having suffered a great deal he rose from the mud of the earth and returned to his God.

In the cathedral of the soul there is more joy over one sinner who repents than over one thousand righteous men who need no repentance.

The fifth of the seven received the elixir of long life in Lemuria eighteen million years ago. The fifth of the seven kept that Lemurian body during the whole Atlantean period and was one of the wise spiritual leaders who led the destinies of millions of human beings of the sunken continent. After the sinking of Atlantis, that Master fell in love with a woman, and later with another. Then he fell; he lost his marvellous body, and became subjected to the terrible wheel of reincarnation and Karma.

Eliphas Levi makes the mistake of commenting on an apocryphal document written by Enoch, and misjudges the Twenty Egregores of the Mountain of the Oath, condemning them dogmatically and branding them as demons.

139

There is something impure in the teachings of Eliphas Levi.

Rudolph Steiner says that Eliphas Levi was reincarnated twice as a priest in a Mexican tribe. That tribe, after having culminated in splendours of wisdom and glory, eventually went into decadence and sorcery. Then that soul who later became Eliphas Levi fed on that impure knowledge. Only in that way can we understand the big mistakes made by Abbot Alphonse Louis Constant (Eliphas Levi). We want to make it clear that we are not saying that Eliphas Levi is a black magician. What we are saying is that there is in his works a great deal of impure knowledge, despite the fact that they have the hallmark of greatness. That is all.

Azazel is an Egregor who did great services to humanity.

Azazel was King Solomon. The bodhisattva of Azazel is now fallen, but it is only natural that in the near future that bodhisattva will rise from the mud of the earth.

Raphael is fallen these days and he is struggling to rise. Raphael is also an Egregor, despite the fact that he does not appear among the Twenty Egregores of the Mountain of the Oath. All the angels of a family, nation, tribe, etc. are Egregores.

In the Theosophical Glossary of H.P. Blavatsky, we find the following:

EGREGORES (from the Greek word 'egregori'). Eliphas Levi calls them 'the chiefs of the souls who are the spirits of energy and action'. Whichever it can mean, the eastern occultists describe the Egregores as beings whose bodies and essences are a tissue of what is called astral light. They are the shadows (or the bodhisattvas) of the higher planetary spirits whose bodies are of the essence of the higher divine light. In the Book of Enoch, that name has been given to the angels who married the daughters of Seth and who had the Giants for children.

The names and symbols of the seven angels of the Eternal have also seven meanings. This has confused many esoterist students.

'*And I saw what appeared to be a sea of glass mixed with fire, and those who had conquered the beast and its image and the number of its name, standing beside the sea of glass with harps of God in their hands.*' (Rev. 15:2).

The liquid, flexible, malleable glass is the christonic semen. Semen is indeed the habitation of fire. Semen is the *vitriol* of the old medieval alchemists.

Those who have conquered the beast can walk full of happiness over the sea of glass, speaking the Lost Speech, speaking in the most pure *orthos* of the Divine Language.

The larynx is the Lyre of Orpheus. We must learn to play the Lyre of Orpheus. We must incarnate the Word. When the Word becomes flesh in us, then we can pluck the Lyre of Orpheus and we can walk in victory over the sea of glass.

Those are the conquerors who have gained the victory over the beast and over the image and the number of its name.

'*And they sing the song of Moses, the servant of God, and the song of the Lamb, saying, "Great and wonderful are your deeds, O Lord God the Almighty! Just and true are your ways, O King of the ages! Who will not fear and glorify your name, O Lord? For you alone are holy. All nations will come and worship you, for your judgements have been revealed."*' (Rev. 15:3-4).

'*And after this I looked, and the temple of the tabernacle of witness in heaven was open, and out of the temple came the seven angels with the seven plagues, robed in pure bright linen, and their chests girded with golden girdles.*' (Rev. 15:5-6).

'*And one of the four living creatures gave the seven angels seven golden bowls full of the wrath of God who lives for ever and ever.*' (Rev. 15:7).

'*And the temple was filled with smoke from the glory of God and from his power, and no one could enter the temple until the seven plagues of the seven angels were ended.*' (Rev. 15:8).

CHAPTER 27

The Seven Bowls Are Poured

'*T*hen I heard a loud voice from the temple telling the seven angels, "Go and pour out on the earth the seven bowls of the wrath of God."' (Rev. 16:1).

'And the first angel (Gabriel) went and poured his bowl on the earth, and foul and evil sores came upon the men who had the mark of the beast and worshipped its image.' (Rev. 16:2).

The present social demoralization, with all its vices, fornication and scandalous cases of adultery, is a foul and evil sore.

All those human beings who have the mark of the beast and who worship the image of the beast have sinned against the goddess Moon. The crimes committed against the goddess Moon are bitterer than death. Everyone gathers the fruit of their bad works. He who sows the wind shall reap the whirlwind. Deserted wives, husbands who are cheated by their adulterous wives, rapes, kidnaps, liquors, etc. All of that is a foul and evil sore. That is the result of the crimes committed against the goddess Moon.

Gabriel is the ruler of the Moon. Nowadays, in these times of the end, there is a great deal of social degeneration, crimes against nature, incurable cancer, mothers who are deserted together with their children, horrible cases of adultery, countless cases of divorce, frightful diseases, cases of uxoricide, etc. All this social wickedness, all these tears, all these orphans are the result of our bad works. All of that is a foul and evil sore. Gabriel, the ruler of the Moon, administers the law and punishes.

The present hour is grave and definitive. Only by entering into the Eightfold Path taught by the Buddha will we be saved. That eightfold path is completely sexual.

The number eight represents the sign of infinity. The number eight symbolizes the two serpents coiling around the spinal cord, the Two Witnesses, the Caduceus of Mercury, the Holy Eight. The pathway is the spine. The Intermediate Path is the spine. That is the path of the razor's edge.

The great Master Francisco A. Propato has said that the sign of infinity is a symbol of the brain, heart and sex of the Genie of the Earth.

The fight is terrible. Brain against sex. Sex against brain. Heart against heart.

Hilarius IX said, *'The fire of the Phlegethon and the water of the Acheron intertwine in the Ninth Sphere, forming the sign of infinity.'*

The eight stages of the Eightfold Path in the Ninth Sphere are the following:

1. Creative understanding.

2. Right intentions.

3. Right speech.

4. Absolute sacrifice.

5. Right behaviour.

6. Absolute chastity.

7. Constant fighting against the black magicians.

8. Supreme patience in all trials and pains.

The Two Witnesses, coiling around the spinal cord, form the Holy Eight. In the Holy Order of Tibet the student is taught about the sign of infinity.

The number of the Logos is 888. If we multiply eight by three, we have the twenty-four vowels of the Great Zodiacal Lyre resounding in all those who incarnated the Cosmic Christ. The

Eightfold Path taught by the Buddha is therefore absolutely sexual. However, the Buddha spoke in a veiled way, because it was then strictly forbidden for the Initiates to divulge the Great Arcanum. The Eightfold Path is the central canal of the spinal cord.

The Caduceus of Mercury is like an eight in shape. That caduceus represents the sign of infinity. That caduceus represents the spine with its two sympathetic cords called Ida and Pingala. The eight stages of the Eightfold Path are found in the spine.

We are in the times of the end, and if we want to get out of this valley of sorrows, we need to enter the Eightfold Path.

There are *four great truths* that have the power to annihilate the ruler of this world:

The first truth is to become absolutely conscious of pain and affliction.

The second tremendous truth is that pain is a child of fornication, and that anyone who spills the semen is a fornicator.

The third truth is that we have an I that must be decapitated and dissolved in order to incarnate the Word.

The fourth truth is that only by practising the A.Z.F. Arcanum can we decapitate and dissolve the ruler of this world.

All those who have decapitated the I can incarnate the Immolated Lamb. In these times of the end we need to incarnate the Word in order to be saved from the great cataclysm. It is urgent to understand the Four Truths. Those who walk in the Eightfold Path become dragons of the Four Truths.

Every dragon of the Four Truths is a Buddha. Listen to me, O Buddhas! You need to incarnate the Christ. Only by renouncing Nirvana for the sake of humanity and working intensely in the Forge of Vulcan (sex) can the Buddhas incarnate the Christ. To the one who knows the word gives power. No one pronounced it, no one will pronounce it, but only the one who has incarnated him. He has to be incarnated!

145

'And the second angel (Raphael) *poured his bowl into the sea, and it became like the blood of a dead man, and every living thing in the sea died.'* (Rev. 16:3).

When we all, the Brothers, investigate this second angel, whose name is Raphael, and this terrible verse, then we see the present time with all its horrors.

That sea symbolizes peoples and multitudes and tongues. Every person in the boat of his own life. Every person in the arcanum of affliction, and when the angel pours his bowl into the sea, the waters become blood.

All the peoples of the earth are bloodstained. Rivers of blood flow through the mountains of pain. There are dictatorships and persecutions everywhere. There are revolutions and death all over the face of the earth. Ones against the others and all against all. There are coups d'etat everywhere. There are frightful gestapos, fearful bodies of police, tears and supreme pain everywhere.

The peoples of the earth are paying the Nemesis, the Karma of their own errors. All the peoples of the earth have been called before the Divine Tribunal. That is the Law. That is Karma.

The waters of life became blood and there is no remedy for this. It is useless to send more prophets to the earth. Humanity detests the prophets. And no one can save this. No one can any longer sort this out. Human evolution is a total failure. The waters have become blood and only cries of supreme pain are heard everywhere.

'And the third angel (Uriel) *poured his bowl into the rivers and the fountains of water, and they became blood.'* (Rev. 16:4). Then the constellation of Cancer will scourge all the fornicators of the earth with its plague (cancer).

'And I heard the angel of the waters say, "You are just, O Holy One, who are and were, for you have judged these things. For men have shed the blood of saints and prophets, and you have given them blood to drink. It is what they deserve!"' (Rev. 16:5-6). And countless diseases will scourge the human

146

rivers and the sexual fountains of the human organism. Radioactivity will produce unknown diseases which science will not be able to cure.

'And I heard the altar say, "Yes, Lord God the Almighty, your judgements are true and just!"' (Rev. 16:7).

'And the fourth angel (Michael) *poured his bowl on the sun, and it was allowed to scorch men with fire. Men were scorched by the fierce heat, and they cursed the name of God, who had power over these plagues, and they did not repent and give him glory.'* (Rev. 16:8-9).

The fourth angel, Michael, has no physical body in these times of the end.

The sun is the symbol of the Cosmic Christ. Christ is love. The antithesis of love is hatred. Know you peoples, multitudes and tongues that hatred becomes a scorching fire. There will be horrible atomic wars — humanity is scorched with living fire. The great cities will turn into ashes, and yet men will curse the name of God who has power over these plagues, and they did not repent and give him glory.

Listen, O peoples! Know that hatred is the most terrible monster that exists on the earth. Who could now save this? Hatred will unleash all the wars, and there will be no remedy. All this has failed. Every man for himself!

'And the fifth angel (Samael) *poured his bowl on the throne of the beast, and its kingdom was plunged into darkness; men gnawed their tongues in anguish, and cursed the God of heaven because of their pain and sores, and they did not repent of their deeds.'* (Rev. 16:10-11).

The fifth of the seven is the one who has suffered most, and he was a fallen master, but he is not fallen any more. The fifth of the seven is now risen. The fifth of the seven poured his bowl on the throne of the beast, and its kingdom plunged into darkness. Millions of human beings already have the mark of the beast on their foreheads and on their hands. Millions of human souls have already separated completely from the Intimate.

The urban life of all the cities and peoples of the world has now been transplanted to the abyss. In the sunken regions of the abyss the human beings continue living in their same systems of urban life; and they buy and sell *'cargo of gold, silver, jewels and pearls, fine linen, purple, silk and scarlet, all kinds of scented wood, all articles of ivory, all articles of costly wood, bronze, iron and marble.'* (Rev. 18:12).

In the abyss the adepts of the shadow live the same urban life to which they are used. The abyss is more material than the physical world, and human beings torment one another even worse than in the physical world. The realm of the abyss has now become darker than ever, and almost the totality of humanity has entered the abyss.

The fifth of the seven and his legions collaborate with the plan of the Logos, and the adepts of the shadow are sinking into the abyss.

Millions of women and distinguished gentlemen who are now living in the world do no longer have the Intimate in them, and they are wicked demons, although they are still reincarnated.

The earth is a failed world. This will be destroyed! No one can save this! The fifth of the seven watches the adepts of the shadow. Many have slandered the fifth of the seven, because he is a watcher.

The adepts of the shadow cursed the God of heaven for their pains and sores, and they did not repent of their deeds.

When the psychological I succeeds in absolutely controlling the four bodies of sin (physical, etheric, astral and mental), then the Intimate withdraws and man becomes a demon. Millions of people who live in the world are now terribly wicked demons. The realm of the beast is now darker than ever.

There is a Divine Bolt within man. That Bolt wants to return to its star that has always smiled at it. The star that guides our interior is a superdivine atom of the Absolute Abstract Space. The kabbalistic name for that atom is the sacred Ain Soph. Know you that the Ain Soph is secretly related to the one-thousand-petalled lotus. The star that guides our interior (Ain Soph) sent its Bolt to the world in order to become conscious of its own happiness. Happiness without consciousness of its own happiness is not happiness. The Bolt had a mineral, vegetable and animal consciousness.

When the Bolt (the Spirit) first incarnated in a savage and primitive human body, it awakened as man and became self-conscious of its own happiness. Then the Bolt could have returned to the star that guides its interior. Unfortunately, in the deep bosom of the maelstrom of the thick forest, wild desire caused the I to come into existence. Nature's instinctive forces trapped man's innocent mind, and the false mirage of desire appeared. Then the I continued reincarnating to satisfy its desires. That is how we became subjected to the law of evolution and Karma.

Experiences and pain made the I complicated. Evolution is a process of complication of energy. The I became stronger and more complicated with experiences. Now it is too late. Millions of people became monstrous demons. Only a tremendous revolution can save us from the abyss. When man dissolves the I, then there is a total revolution. When man is able to dissolve the I, then he can stop suffering. Pain is the result of our bad works. Pain belongs to Satan, because he is the one doing the works of evil. The Absolute Abstract Space, the Universal Spirit of Life, is absolute happiness, supreme peace and abundance.

Those who make a mysticism out of pain are masochists. Satan was and is the creator of pain. Pain corrupts man because pain is satanic. No one can become liberated through pain. We need to become alchemists. Through Alchemy the I is dissolved. The root of the I is desire. Desire is transmuted through Alchemy. If you want to annihilate desire, you have to transmute it. Sexual desire is transmuted into will, and will is fire. The desire of accumulation (covetousness) is transmuted into altruism. Anger (frustrated desire) is transmuted into sweetness. Envy (frustrated desire) is transmuted into joy for others' good. The words of desire are transmuted into words of wisdom, etc.

Analyse all human faults and you will see that they are based on desire. Transmute desire with the help of Alchemy, and desire will be annihilated. Anyone who annihilates desire dissolves the I. Anyone who dissolves the I is saved from the abyss and returns to his inner star that has always smiled at him. Only with Holy Alchemy can we dissolve the I. The foundation of Alchemy is the A.Z.F. Arcanum. Angels, archangels, seraphim, powers, thrones, etc. are the exact result of tremendous inner revolutions.

We have already gone through involution (the descent of the Spirit into matter). We have already suffered horribly in the stage of evolution (process of complication of energy). What is now urgent is a total revolution (the dissolution of the I). Only through inner revolutions can we return to the Superdivine Atom little by little, going through the angelic, archangelic, seraphic, logoic, etc. states, until the Bolt finally fuses with its star (Ain Soph), which shines with happiness.

The abyss is terribly painful. The horrible antithesis of Ain Soph is the abyss.

The fifth of the seven has poured his bowl on the throne of the beast, and its kingdom has now become darker than ever. Woe to the dwellers of the earth!

'*And the sixth angel* (Zachariel) *poured his bowl on the great river Euphrates, and its water was dried up, to prepare the way for the kings from the east.*' (Rev. 16:12). The Euphrates is one of the rivers of Eden. The first river is the elemental earth of the wise (the tattva prithvi). The second is the elemental water (the tattva apas). The third is the elemental air (the tattva vayu). The fourth is the elemental fire of the wise (the tattva tejas).

All the elements are summed up in fire. Everything comes out of fire and everything goes back to fire. The creative fire of the Holy Spirit is the river Euphrates. Zachariel pours his bowl on the river Euphrates, and then the river dries up. The Anglo-Saxons and the French are loosing the power to create.

150

The Euphrates is drying up and women are becoming sterile. Now in England and France statistics are recording a higher death rate and a lower birth rate. Thousands of souls are entering the abyss daily. Those souls are not given a body any more. The result then is a lesser amount of births and a greater amount of deaths. The river Euphrates is drying up to prepare the way for the sacred kings from the Inner East.

'And I saw, issuing from the mouth of the dragon and from the mouth of the beast and from the mouth of the false prophet (materialistic science), *three foul spirits like frogs. For they are demonic spirits, performing signs, who go abroad to the kings of the whole world, to assemble them for battle on the great day of God the Almighty.'* (Rev. 16:13-14).

Those three foul spirits like frogs constitute the psychological I of every human being. These are Core, Dathan and Abiram. These are the three traitors. These are the three rebels that are within us. The first is the rebel against nature. The second is the rebel against divine science. The third is·the rebel against truth.

The first is the demon of desire. The second is the demon of the mind. The third is the demon of the bad will. The first is in the astral body. The second is in the mental body. The third is in the body of the will (causal body).

The three of them are the three-headed black dragon. These are Sebal, Hortelut and Stokin — the three traitors of Hiram Abiff. These three foul spirits are the I, the ego, the myself. These three foul spirits perform signs: H-bombs, planes, rockets, mechanical wonders with which to deceive people, and to assemble them for battle. These three foul spirits invent materialistic theories: dialectic materialism, historic materialism, etc.

These three foul spirits are experts in materialistic science, and laugh at everything having a spiritual flavour.

These three demons perform wonders in chemistry, in physics, in medicine, and deceive people with false miracles and wonders.

'See, I am coming like a thieve! Blessed are those who are awake, keeping their (sacred) *garments* (without losing them) *so that they may not go naked and be seen exposed!'* (Rev. 16:15).

'And they assembled them at the place which is called in Hebrew Armageddon.' (Rev. 16:16). Armageddon is the atomic war. Soon men will use small pocket weapons with atomic missiles to hurt and to disintegrate atomic bombs and rockets loaded with nuclear explosives in space. The whole atmosphere will become filled with deadly radioactive particles. Millions of flying discs, crewed by other planetary humanities, are watching us. The day of the tremendous cataclysm is drawing near, and the humanities of other planets are watching us.

'And the seventh angel (Oriphiel) *poured his bowl into the air, and a loud voice came out of the temple, from the throne, saying, "It is done!"'* (Rev. 16:17). The angel of Saturn swings his mortal sickle on the face of the earth and everything is consummated.

A world is approaching the earth, and when it crashes with it, everything will have been consummated. That collision of worlds will be exceedingly frightful.

'And there were flashes of lightening, voices, peals of thunder, and a great earthquake such as had never been since men were on the earth, so great was that earthquake.' (Rev. 16:18).

It is now when men will be known! It is now when we will know who is who! And the learned ignoramuses will bite dust. And the authoritarian wiseacres of some schools of rogues will swallow mud. And the false prophets will exhibit their shame in the abyss of the failed ones.

May the earth shake! May the wolf of the Law howl!

It is now indeed when men will be known, and we will see many men crying like harlots! The time to show consideration is over.

Those who killed the prophets will find themselves naked, and those who were applauded by the great harlot will drink bitter bile. The barbarians gave the saints honey with hemlock to drink. Now the Law will scourge them with scorpions. May the catastrophe come! It is now indeed! It is now when we will know who is who! Now men will be known!

'*And the great city was split into three parts, and the cities of the nations fell, and God remembered great Babylon, to make her drain the cup of the fury of his wrath. And every island fled away, and no mountains were to be found* (the earth swallowed them).' (Rev. 16:19-20).

That is what the great harlot deserves! The saints said what they had to say! Now, may the tragedy come!

The hour of the great cataclysm has come!

May the Law come! May the hurricane roar! May the earth shake!

The time to be awaiting has passed. Now... the tragedy!

This is how the Avatar of Aquarius speaks: Frankly! Sincerely! This time the righteous will not pay for the sinners. That happened once, and that time has passed.

Before the great cataclysm the righteous will be secretly saved. Let us remember Lot, taken out of the cursed city. Let us remember Elijah, caught up to heaven in a chariot of fire. The righteous will be taken out of the great Babylon before the great cataclysm.

Many flying discs will come to the earth. Other planetary humanities are watching us. They know the terrible hour in which we live.

Shortly before the final burst (the great cataclysm), the righteous will be secretly helped. They will be taken away as Elijah was taken in a chariot of fire. They will live in another planet. And the mountains will blow up into the air, broken into pieces. And the earth will spew out fire and water. The earth will become a mass of fire and water.

The sign? The day? The hour?: When there will be spaceships able to arrive at other planets. When men will be ready to conquer and dominate other planetary humanities by force. When they will like to repeat their bloody historic conquests in other planets.

Be all the time alert and watchful.

Every step man takes in the conquest of space is getting him closer and closer to the great cataclysm.

Before the great cataclysm there will be frightful and exceedingly terrible atomic wars.

'And great hailstones, each weighing about a talent, dropped from heaven on men, until men cursed God for the plague of the hail, so fearful was that plague.' (Rev. 16:21).

CHAPTER 28

The Harlot and the Beast

'*A*nd one of the seven angels who had the seven bowls came and said to me, "Come, I will show you the judgement of the great harlot* (humanity), *who is seated on many waters, with whom the kings of the earth have committed fornication, and with the wine of whose fornication the dwellers of the earth have become drunk."*' (Rev. 17:1-2).

'*And he carried me away in the Spirit into a wilderness, and I saw a woman sitting on a scarlet beast* (the great beast, whose number is 666), *which was full of blasphemous names, and it had seven heads and ten horns.*' (Rev. 17:3). The seven heads of the beast are the seven capital sins, and the ten horns mean that the beast comes up out of the abyss and will fall back into the abyss.

'*And the woman* (the great harlot) *was clothed in purple and scarlet* (that is how it is symbolized in the inner worlds), *and adorned with gold and jewels and pearls, holding in her hand a golden cup full of abominations and the impurities of her fornication.*' (Rev. 17:4).

'*And on her forehead was written a name of mystery: Babylon the great, mother of harlots and of earth's abominations.*' (Rev. 17:5).

'*And I saw the woman, drunk with the blood of the saints and the blood of the martyrs of Jesus, and when I saw her I was greatly marvelled.*' (Rev. 17:6).

'But the angel said to me, "Why are you so marvelled? I will tell you the mystery of the woman, and of the beast with seven heads and ten horns that carries her.' (Rev. 17:7).

'"The beast that you saw was, and is not, and is to ascend from the abyss and go to perdition; and the dwellers of the earth whose names have not been written in the book of life from the foundation of the world, will be marvelled when they see the beast, because it was and is not and is to come.' (Rev. 17:8).

'"This calls for a mind with wisdom: the seven heads are seven mountains on which the woman is seated.' (Rev. 17:9).

The seven capital sins: anger, covetousness, lust, envy, pride, sloth and gluttony, are related to the seven sub-planes or dark regions of the abyss. Those are the seven mountains on which the great harlot is seated.

'"And they are also seven kings (the seven kings of Eden), *five of whom have fallen, one is, and the other has not yet come, and when he comes he must remain only a little while.'* (Rev. 17:10).

The five lower principles: soul, mind, astral body, etheric body and physical body, are fallen. Man is fallen. The sixth principle, the soul-consciousness or Buddhi never falls, and it will govern in the sixth race.

When the reign of the seventh principle comes, it will remain only a little while. Then there will be a divine race: the seventh race. The seventh principle is the Intimate.

'"As for the beast that was and is not, it is an eighth but it belongs to the seven, and it goes to perdition.' (Rev. 17:11).

The beast that was and is not, it is an eighth. It is the shadow of the seven sephiroth; it is the abyss.

'"And the ten horns that you saw are ten kings who have not yet received royal power, but they are to receive authority as kings for one hour, together with the beast.' (Rev. 17:12).

The ten horns of the tragic wheel will go up and down; they will turn with the wheel of compensation. They come up out of the abyss, impose their authority and rule as ten kings, and then they will fall back into the abyss when the wheel of Nemesis completes its fatal turn.

'*"These* (the ten horns) *are of one mind and give over their power and authority to the beast.'* (Rev. 17:13).

'*"They will make war on the Lamb, and the Lamb will conquer them, for he is Lord of lords and King of kings, and those with him are called and chosen and faithful."'* (Rev. 17:14).

'*And he said to me, "The waters that you saw, where the harlot is seated, are peoples and multitudes and nations and tongues.'* (Rev. 17:15).

'*"And the ten horns that you saw, they and the beast will hate the harlot; they will make her desolate and naked, and will devour her flesh and burn her up with fire.'* (Rev. 17:16). When the tragic wheel of compensation turns fatally, the harlot will be made desolate and naked, and the ten tragic horns will devour her flesh and will burn her up with the fire of fornication amidst the darkness of the abyss.

'*"For God has put it into their hearts to carry out his purpose by being of one mind and giving over their royal power to the beast, until the words of God will be fulfilled.'* (Rev. 17:17).

'*"And the woman that you saw is the great city which has domination over the kings of the earth.'* (Rev. 17:18).

The tragic great city is Babylon the Great, the mother of all fornication and abominations of the earth — the wicked modern civilization.

Woe to those who will not listen to the word written in this book!

Woe to the dwellers of the earth!

Woe, woe, to those who betray the Work of my Father!

CHAPTER 29

Fallen Is Babylon

'*After this I saw another angel coming down from heaven, having great authority, and the earth was made bright with his splendour.*' (Rev. 18:1).

'*And he called out with a mighty voice, "Fallen, fallen is Babylon the great!* (The wicked civilization of this race). *It has become a dwelling place of demons, a haunt of every foul spirit, a haunt of every foul and hateful bird.*' (Rev. 18:2). Birds of crime, vultures of war, birds of prey and hatred, etc.

'*"For all nations have drunk the wine of her fornication, and the kings of the earth* (the magnates of the world) *have committed fornication with her, and the merchants of the earth have grown rich from the power of her luxury."*' (Rev. 18:3).

'*Then I heard another voice from heaven saying, "Come out of her, my people* (people initiated into the christic mysteries), *so that you do not take part in her sins, and so that you do not share in her plagues.*' (Rev. 18:4).

And the righteous will be secretly taken out of this great city. And they will be taken away in interplanetary ships before the great cataclysm.

The wicked dwellers of the earth will perish, '*"for her sins are heaped high as heaven, and God has remembered her iniquities.*' (Rev. 18:5).

The righteous will live in another planet while the earth goes through a great geological transformation. Later they will

159

return to this world to form the sixth race. Babylon the Great will be turned into ashes and blood.

'"*Render to her as she herself has rendered, and repay her double for her deeds; mix a double draught for her in the cup she mixed. As she glorified herself and lived luxuriously, so give her a like measure of torment and mourning. Since in her heart she says, 'I sit as a queen, I am no widow, and I will never see mourning.'* (Rev. 18:6-7).

'"*So her plagues will come in a single day, pestilence and mourning and famine, and she will be burnt with fire, for mighty is the Lord God who judges her.*"' (Rev. 18:8). The great harlot gathers the fruit of her evil works. He who sows the wind shall reap the whirlwind. That is the law. The great harlot will reap the fruit of her evil deeds.

The great harlot will be burnt with the fire of the atomic war and with the cosmic fire which, with the planetary collision, will turn the world into a mass of fire and water vapour.

All this will be fulfilled in the New Aquarian Era. You will see frightful things before the final cataclysm. The Vatican will be destroyed. The great cities of the world will be reduced to ashes, blood and ruins. Money will be worthless, and the human beings will kill one another over a piece of stale bread. The great Babylon will be turned into dust.

'*And the kings of the earth* (the magnates of gold and silver, the oil tycoons and the vultures of war), *who committed fornication and lived in luxury with her, will weep and wail over her when they see the smoke of her burning; they will stand far off* (trying to flee from the disaster) *in fear of her torment, and say, "Alas! alas! you great city, you mighty city, Babylon!* (The modern civilization). *For in one hour your judgement has come.*"' (Rev. 18:9-10).

'*And the merchants of the earth weep and mourn for her, since no one buys their cargo any more, cargo of gold, silver, jewels and pearls, fine linen, purple, silk and scarlet, all kinds of scented wood, all articles of ivory, all articles of costly wood, bronze, iron and marble, cinnamon, spice, incense, myrrh, frankincense, wine, oil, fine flour and wheat, cattle and sheep, horses and chariots, slaves and human souls.'* (Rev. 18:11-13). The merchants of the earth make money even with men's souls.

'*"And the fruit for which your soul longed has gone from you, and all your dainties and your splendour are lost to you, never to be found again."'* (Rev. 18:14). The atomic war will destroy everything.

Until the final catastrophe comes, *'the merchants of these wares, who gained wealth from her, will stand far off* (they will flee from the cities), *in fear of her torment, weeping and mourning aloud, "Alas, alas, for the great city* (the modern civilization) *that was clothed in fine linen, in purple and scarlet, adorned with gold, with jewels, and with pearls!'* (Rev. 18:15-16).

'*"For in one hour all this wealth has been laid waste." And all shipmasters and seafarers, sailors and all whose trade is on the sea, stood far off and cried out as they saw the smoke of her burning, "What city was like the great city?"'* (Rev. 18:17-18).

'And they threw dust on their heads, as they wept and mourned, crying out, "Alas, alas, the great city, where all who had ships at sea grew rich by her wealth! For in one hour (the hour of Karma and punishment) *she has been laid waste."'* (Rev. 18:19).

'Rejoice over her, O heaven, O saints and apostles and prophets, for God has given judgement for you against her!' (Rev. 18:20).

The thunderbolt of Cosmic Justice will fall upon this wicked civilization of vipers, and there will be no remedy.

'And a mighty angel took up a stone like a great millstone (the philosopher's stone) *and threw it into the sea* (the christonic semen), *saying* (the prophecy is sealed), *"With such violence Babylon the great city* (the modern civilization) *will be thrown down, and will be found no more."'* (Rev. 18:21).

'*And the sound of harpists and minstrels, of flautists and trumpeters, will be heard in you no more; and a craftsman of any craft will be found in you no more; and the sound of the millstone will be heard in you no more.*' (Rev. 18:22).

'*And the light of a lamp will shine in you no more; and the voice of bridegroom and bride will be heard in you no more, for your merchants were the great men of the earth* (the great business tycoons), *and all nations were deceived by your sorcery.*' (Rev. 18:23).

Sorcery is the golden calf. Sorcery is the present idolatry. Sorcery is the scepticism of dialectic materialism. Sorcery is the exploitation of souls. Sorcery is black magic, witchcraft, etc.

On account of all this, Babylon the Great, the mother of all fornication and abominations of the earth, will be destroyed.

'*And in her was found the blood of prophets and of saints, and of all who has been killed on the earth.*' (Rev. 18:24).

CHAPTER 30

The Buddha Maitreya

*'A*fter this I heard what seemed to be the loud voice of a great multitude in heaven, saying, "Hallelujah! Salvation and glory and power belong to our God.' (Rev. 19:1).

'"For his judgements are true and just; he has judged the great harlot* (mankind) *who corrupted the earth with her fornication, and he has avenged on her the blood of his servants* (initiates)."' (Rev. 19:2).

'Once more they said, "Hallelujah! And the smoke from her goes up for ever and ever."' (Rev. 19:3).

'And the twenty-four elders* (of the Zodiac) *and the four living creatures* (of sexual alchemy) *fell down and worshipped God* (Truth), *who is seated on the* (inner) *throne, saying, "Amen. Hallelujah!"'* (Rev. 19:4).

'And from the throne* (which we have in the depths of our Being) *came a voice saying, "Praise our* (Inner) *God, all you his servants, you who fear him, small and great."'* (Rev. 19:5).

'Then I heard what seemed to be the voice of a great multitude, like the sound of many waters* (the seminal waters) *and like the sound of mighty thunder-peals* (the voice of the gods), *saying, "Hallelujah! For the Lord our God the Almighty* (who is within us) *reigns.'* (Rev. 19:6).

'"Let us rejoice and exult and give him the glory, for the marriage of the Lamb has come, and his bride* (the soul) *has made herself ready.'* (Rev. 19:7).

'*"And it has been granted to her to be clothed with fine linen* (the masters' robe), *bright and pure."* For the fine linen is the *righteous deeds of the saints.'* (Rev. 19:8).

'And he said to me, *"Write this: Blessed are those who are invited to the marriage supper of the Lamb."* And he said to me, *"These are true words of God."'* (Rev. 19:9).

'Then I fell down at his feet to worship him, but he said to me, *"You must not do that! I am a fellow servant with you and your brothers who hold the testimony of Jesus. Worship God* (who is your Inner God).*" For the testimony of Jesus is the spirit of prophecy.'* (Rev. 19:10).

'*And I saw heaven opened, and behold, a white horse! The one who sat on it* (the fifth of the seven) *is called Faithful and True, and in righteousness he judges and makes war.'* (Rev. 19:11). The one who is writing this book bears witness to this prophecy, because he is the servant-bodhisattva of the fifth of the seven.

The Son speaks the word of the Father and bears witness to the Father. The Father is one with the Son. The Son is one with the Father.

The Son does not consider himself worthy to untie the sandals of the Father. Only the Father is perfect.

The Father rejoices in the Son, and the Son rejoices in the Father.

The Buddha Maitreya Samael is the Kalki Avatar of the New Era. He is the rider of the white horse. However, his son, the poor servant who is writing this Message of Aquarius, does not really consider himself worthy even to kiss the sacred feet of the Father. The Buddha Maitreya shines with glory, and his son kneels down.

'*And his eyes are like a flame of fire, and on his head are many diadems, and he has a name inscribed which no one knows but himself* (because it is written in characters of the Language of the Light). *He is clothed in a robe dipped in blood* (during

164

the battle against the Black Lodge, in the suprasensible worlds), *and the name by which he is called is the Word of God.'* (Rev. 19:12-13). The Avatar of the New Era is a Word.

'And the armies of heaven, clothed in fine linen, white and pure (because they are Masters), *followed him on white horses* (the cavalry of Nirvana).' (Rev. 19:14).

'And from his mouth issues a sharp sword (speech) *with which to smite the nations* (to smite the demons — people separated from the Inner God), *and he* (the Word) *will rule them with a rod of iron* (in the abyss), *and he will tread the wine press of the fury of the wrath of God the Almighty.'* (Rev. 19:15). The adepts of the shadow have fought against the Word, but the Word treads the wine press of the fury and throws them into the abyss.

'And on his robe and on his thigh he has a name inscribed (in sacred characters on a ribbon), *King of kings and Lord of lords.'* (Rev. 19:16).

The power of the King is not on the forehead. The power of the King is in the sexual organs. The sceptre of the sacred kings, the two pillars of the temple and the cross of the Redeemer are made out of the wood of the Tree of Good and Evil. This is the Tree of Knowledge (sex). When a man and a woman are sexually united, something is created. When we receive the sacred fire of the Holy Spirit, we become kings and lords of nature.

Kundalini is the fire of the Holy Spirit. Kundalini develops, evolves, and progresses within the aura of the Maha Chohan. The Maha Chohan is the Holy Spirit, the Third Logos, whom we find in the Forge of Vulcan. That forge is sex. Only through sexual magic (the A.Z.F. Arcanum) does Kundalini awaken.

The great German sage Krumm Heller says the following in the Eighth Lesson of his Zodiacal Course: *'Instead of a sexual intercourse ending in orgasm, man and woman must reflexively lavish sweet caresses, words of love and delicate fondling on each other, keeping their minds constantly away from animal sexuality, sustaining the most pure spirituality, as if the act were a true religious ceremony.*

'Nevertheless, man can and must introduce his penis and keep it in the female sexual organ (in the vulva), *so that a divine sensation can come upon both of them — a sensation that can last for hours on end. The man must remove it just when the spasm draws near, in order to avoid the seminal ejaculation. In this way they will want to caress each other more and more.'* Semen must not be spilt either inside the vulva, nor outside it, nor on the sides, nor anywhere.

Dr. Krumm Heller goes on to say the following: '*This can be repeated as many times as one wants to, without ever experiencing tiredness, for quite the opposite, it is the magic key to becoming daily rejuvenated, keeping one's body healthy and prolonging one's life, since it is a fountain of health, with this constant magnetization.*

'*We know that in ordinary magnetism, the magnetizer communicates fluids to the subject, and if the magnetic forces of the first are developed, he can heal the second. The transmission of magnetic fluid is usually done through hands or through eyes. But it is necessary to say that there is no other more powerful conductor, a thousand times more powerful, a thousand times superior to others, than the male member and the vulva, as organs of reception.*

'*If many people practise this, then force and success will spread around them on anyone with whom they have a business or social relationship. But in this act of sublime and divine magnetization that we are referring to, both man and woman magnetize each other, the one being to the other like a musical instrument, which, when it is played, sends out prodigious sounds of mysterious and sweet harmonies. The strings of that instrument are scattered all over the body; and lips and fingers are the main players of it, provided that the most absolute purity presides over this act, which is the one making us magicians in that supreme moment.*'

In these paragraphs of M. Huiracocha is the key to awakening Kundalini. This is the A.Z.F. Arcanum. This is the Great Arcanum.

When Cazotte, the great French poet, wrote his famous book entitled *The Loving Devil*, he was then visited by a man who came wrapped in a cloak. That mysterious personage was Master Zanoni. Then the mysterious visitor made some secret greetings which Cazotte could not understand. Cazotte was not an initiate, but Zanoni initiated him.

The style in which *The Loving Devil* was written is close to the A.Z.F. Arcanum.

Zanoni told the Great Arcanum to the great French poet from mouth to ear. We still remember the terrible death prophecies at the famous banquet of Cazotte.

Some initiates wanted to reveal the Great Arcanum and others opposed to it. Cazotte, exalted by wisdom, prophesized exile for some, and scaffold, suicide, dagger, poison for others, and finally, he prophesized his own death at the scaffold. All the prophecies of Cazotte were fulfilled with astonishing accuracy.

Another marvellous personage was the powerful and enigmatic Count Cagliostro. This man, the age of whom is impenetrable, is a true Master who has the elixir of long life. No one can have this elixir without having worked first with the A.Z.F. Arcanum.

Cagliostro swallowed soil in the grave and was able to get out of the tomb because he had received the elixir of long life. Cagliostro practised sexual magic intensely. Cagliostro was a disciple of Count Saint Germain.

Cagliostro was an alchemist. He transmuted led into gold and made legitimate diamonds. This Master was known in different places by different names. At times he was known by a name in one country and by other names in other countries. He was known by the names of Tis-chio, Milissa, Belmonte, D'anna, Fenix, Pellegrini, Balsamo, Mesmer, Harut and Cagliostro, as it is recorded in the minutes of the famous trial over *The Queen's Necklace*, which is the title of a work by Alexander Dumas. Ragon commits the crime of slandering the Great Copt. Eliphas Levi too slanders Count Cagliostro, accusing him of being a black magician. In Germany the Great Copt shared quarters with the famous Schrader, and in England with the illustrious Theosophist George Costom.

With his science of the philosopher's stone, Cagliostro saved the life of the Archbishop of Rohan.

The Baroness of Oberkirch told the following about the Great Copt: 'He was not absolutely beautiful, but I never saw a physiognomy like his. His look, rather than profound, was unearthly. I could not define the expression of his eyes. They were ice and fire at the same time, with an irresistible power of influence — now attracting, now repelling.'

In Strasbourg he had many alchemist disciples. Cagliostro was tried by the Inquisition, locked up in the Bastille, and later in the Leone Fortress.

The Inquisition condemned him to death, but the enigmatic and powerful Count Cagliostro disappeared from the prison mysteriously.

Death could not defeat Cagliostro. Cagliostro is still alive with his same physical body, because when a Master has swallowed soil in the grave he becomes a Lord of the living and the dead.

No one can reach this initiatory level without the secret practice of sexual magic. Anyone who rejects the Great Arcanum is a real fool.

The great old initiates suffered a great deal, and many of them perished during the secret trials when they aspired to the supreme secret of the Great Arcanum. Now we are giving the A.Z.F. Arcanum publicly printed in this book. Those who reject this precious treasure are imbeciles.

Another initiate who became realized through sexual magic was Saint Germain. Count Saint Germain, the Master of Cagliostro, rejuvenated himself at will, and appeared and disappeared instantly when least expected. Count Saint Germain was even able to pass himself off as a dead person and to get into the grave in order to later get out of it with his body in the Jinas state.

These masters who swallowed soil usually do their missions in some country and then they pass themselves off as dead in order to close a chapter of their immortal lives. According to the memories of an aristocratic lady who was contemporary of Louis XV, Saint Germain appeared to her in a complete young appearance until 1723, many years after his death, to predict the French Revolution and the tragic death of Louis XVI. Saint Germain then pointed to the incompetent French ministers and defied their anger by making himself invisible at will and unseizable.

Saint Germain was the rival musician of Paganini. Paganini is a black magician.

Saint Germain has the gift of tongues. He speaks all the languages of the world correctly. This Great Master was a counsellor to kings and scholars. He could read in closed sheets of paper. He appeared and disappeared like a flash of lightening. He transmuted lead into gold, and made diamonds through vivifying coal. He was thought to have been born in Jerusalem and to be over two thousand or three thousand years old. We know that Count Saint Germain is still alive with his same physical body. That Great Master worked with the A.Z.F. Arcanum, that is, he practised sexual magic intensely. He owes his power to it. That is why he received the elixir of long-life. Saint Germain works with the ray of world politics. It is a pity that Marie Antoinette would not listen to the advice of Saint Germain.

Cagliostro was the best disciple of Saint Germain. Cagliostro lived in the time of Jesus Christ. He was a friend of Cleopatra in Egypt. He worked for Catherine de Medici. He was Count Fenix, etc. Cagliostro, the disciple of Altotas, is still alive with his same physical body, without death having been able to cut the thread of his precious existence.

Saint Germain was in Europe before the Second World War, and then he returned to his sanctuary in Tibet. The King is not on the forehead but in the sexual organs.

All the disciplines of Yoga — the whole Kriya — culminate in the supreme secret of the Great Arcanum. When a yogi is ready, he receives the A.Z.F. Arcanum from mouth to ear. It is the duty of the Holy Order of Tibet to reveal, from mouth to ear, the Great Arcanum to the yogi who is ready.

That order is made up of two hundred and one members. Its Staff has seventy two Brahmans. Supreme meditation and absolute adoration lead us to ecstasy (shamadi). Every master of shamadi (ecstasy) is an enlightened being. We must know, however, that enlightenment is one thing and realization is another different thing. During his states of supreme adoration, a master of shamadi (ecstasy) can uncoop his mind, which is normally cooped in the I, and experience Truth. However, that does not mean to incarnate Truth. After the ecstasy the mind becomes cooped in the I again, and the mystic continues in his same tragic and painful life. Only by incarnating Truth there is a total revolution in man. Those who want to incarnate Truth need to build the temple on the living stone. That living stone is sex.

The temple of wisdom has seven pillars. Those are the seven degrees of power of the fire. There are seven serpents: two groups made up of three serpents, with the sublime crowning of the seventh tongue of fire, which unites us to the One, to the Law, to the Father.

The first serpent belongs to the physical body. The second belongs to the vital body. The third belongs to the astral body. The fourth belongs to the mental body. The fifth belongs to the body of will. The sixth belongs to the buddhic body, and the seventh belongs to the Intimate. These are the seven scales of knowledge. The seven serpents are not raised simultaneously all together. The Magistery of Fire is very difficult and one progresses by degrees.

First we have to raise the first serpent, then the second, later the third, and so on. The yogi who does not practise the A.Z.F. Arcanum is a garden with no water. Practise yoga, but work with the Great Arcanum in the Magistery of Fire.

If you, dear reader, suppose that there may be some other way to attain the development, evolution and progress of Kundalini, Samael Aun Weor, the Buddha Maitreya of the New Aquarian Era, solemnly swears that you are absolutely wrong. Any other way, opposite or different to sex, has never been known in any school of mysteries in this planet earth or in any other planet of infinite space.

If you are now an old woman; if you cannot have sexual contact any more. If you are now an old man; if you are ill; if you understand that your physical vehicle is not useful any more to work with the A.Z.F. Arcanum; then, train in astral projection, learn to project yourself consciously in your astral body.

Prepare my son through concentration, meditation and adoration. Be chaste in thought, word and deed. Understand your errors. Annihilate not only desire, but even the very shadow of desire. Prepare my son through creative understanding, and make your work with the A.Z.F. Arcanum ready for your next reincarnation.

Are you old? Are you disable? Then do not loose heart, my beloved son. Do not fill yourself with inaction. In your future reincarnation you will be able to work with the A.Z.F. Arcanum and you will become a god.

However, if you are full of youth; if you are not impotent; if you are a complete man, and you reject the Great Arcanum, so that you can continue fornicating, hiding in the speculations of your mind, how wretched you are! Woe to you! Woe, woe, woe! it would have been better for you not to have been born, because now you will tumble down into the abyss inevitably.

That sophism that says that there are many paths to reach God is absolutely false. Our adorable Saviour only taught us about one narrow path and one narrow door, and he said:

'Strive to enter through the narrow door (sex), for many, I tell you, will seek to enter and will not be able. When once the householder has risen up and shut the door, you will begin to stand outside and to knock at the door, saying, "Lord, open to

us." He will answer you, "I do not know where you come from." Then you will begin to say, "We ate and drank in your presence, and you taught in our streets." But he will say, "I tell you, I do not know where you come from; depart from me, all you workers of iniquity!" There you will weep and gnash your teeth, when you see Abraham and Isaac and Jacob and all the prophets in the Kingdom of God and you yourselves thrust out.'

Those who suppose that they can incarnate the Word without the A.Z.F. Arcanum are ignorant. Akasha is the agent of sound. Kundalini is akashic. Without akasha the Word cannot be incarnated, because akasha is the agent of sound. We have to raise the akashic serpent in order to incarnate the Word. Kundalini (akashic fire) becomes creative with the power of speech. Kundalini is the vehicle of the creative word. The creative energy of the Maha Chohan is sexual, and it speaks in the creative larynx. Without the A.Z.F. Arcanum no one can incarnate the Word.

The fifth of the seven, the Word of Aquarius, says to you: *'The King is not on the forehead. The King is in the sexual organs.'*

In the depths of all schools of mysteries lies the Great Arcanum. If you reject the Great Arcanum, how wretched you are! Woe, woe, woe! If your mind is full of theories and you throw away this book saying, 'This book is just another book, as the many I have read before.' Woe to you! Woe, woe, woe! You have rejected the Word. You have insulted the Logos. You have signed your own death sentence, and you will tumble down into the abyss. We are not threatening, dear reader; we are just warning.

Life started its return towards the Great Light. The Final Judgement was already done, and the times of the end have already come. Those unable to raise their serpents along their spinal canals will not be able to ascend with the life that returns to the Absolute, and they will sink into the abyss. They will become demons.

'And I saw an angel standing in the sun, and with a loud voice he called to all the birds that fly in mid-heaven, "Come, gather for the great supper of God, to eat the flesh of kings, the flesh of captains, the flesh of mighty men, the flesh of horses and their riders, and the flesh of all men, both free and slave, both small and great."' (Rev. 19:17-18).

The atomic war and the great cataclysm that are coming will destroy all men: both free and slave, both small and great.

'And I saw the beast and the kings of the earth with their armies gathered to make war against the one who sits on the horse and against his army.' (Rev. 19:19).

The dark legions began to enter Avitchi (the abyss) after the final judgement that was done in 1950. Then great battles started in the astral and mental worlds. And the beast and the adepts of the shadow of the great Black Lodge gathered to make war against the one who sits on the horse (the Word) and against his army.

The bodhisattva who is writing this book bears witness to these battles which the Black Lodge has launched against him who is his Father who is in secret.

To do the final judgement and to send the adepts of the shadow to the abyss were both urgent. These battles that are taking place in the inner worlds will have an effect on the physical world with atomic wars and frightful catastrophes.

'And the beast was captured (in the abyss), *and with it the false prophet* (materialistic intellectualism), *who in its presence had performed the signs* (with his false miracles and wonders, such as hydrogen bombs, atomic bombs, amazing inventions, and finally, his tower of Babel), *by which he deceived those who had received the mark of the beast* (the horns) *and those who worshipped its image* (materialistic science). *These two were thrown alive into the lake of fire that burns with sulphur.'* (Rev. 19:20). That lake of fire that burns with sulphur is the fire of passion and of disaster; it is the abyss, Avitchi, the eighth sunken sphere, nature's atomic hells.

'And the rest were killed by the sword of the one who sits on the horse, the sword that issues from his mouth, and all the birds were gorged with their flesh.' (Rev. 19:21).

When someone who has a body enters the abyss, the Antakarana breaks between the fourth and fifth human principles. Those quaternaries that separate from the spiritual Triad are demons.

When a person is very wicked, his Spirit abandons him.

Those people who have no spirit are demons. When the Spirit definitively leaves the body, that person experiences death, even though he or she is still alive. Then that Spirit is recorded in the book of the disincarnated.

Currently there are many people who no longer have the Spirit (the Intimate). Every person who loses the Intimate becomes a demon. Every demon belongs to the abyss. All those who make war against the Word are killed by the terrible sword which he has in his mouth. All these tragedies, all these catastrophes, all these prophecies, all these cataclysms have a very solid foundation. That foundation is the return of life towards the Absolute.

Those unable to raise the serpent on the rod cannot return to the Absolute, because the return is internal and is based on every step taken by the serpent. The serpent must ascend the thirty-three degrees of the spinal cord.

We have to return ascending through the seven scales of knowledge. We have to return through every one of the seven degrees of power of the fire. We cannot return through theories, because none of us is a child of any theory. Every one of us is a child of a man and of a woman.

This is a sexual question, because we exist thanks to sex. Those who make the mistake of rejecting the A.Z.F. Arcanum will sink into the abyss inevitably. If someone does not want to sink into the abyss, they must start to ascend the sevenfold scale of the ardent fire.

Remember that the abyss is full of people with good intentions.

Remember that the abyss is full of people who think that they are perfect and holy. Many fornicating mystics will enter the abyss.

Those who say: 'I will not practise the A.Z.F. Arcanum.' 'I will continue with my religion.' 'My school is better.' 'My system is a better system.' 'There are other paths...' They will sink into the abyss, because when they run away from the door of Eden (sex), then they will come upon the door of the abyss.

We went out of Eden through the narrow door of sex, and only through that door can we return to Eden. Eden is sex itself.

The return of life towards the Absolute means the fall of the Great Babylon, the catastrophe and the final disaster.

In a remote past we the Brothers of the Temple taught the A.Z.F. Arcanum to the humanity of the ancient Earth-Moon. Then those who accepted the Great Arcanum rose to the angelic state. In those times of the ancient Earth-Moon, we made the same warnings. Our work was carried out when the lunar humanity had reached the age in which the earth's present humanity is now. Life then started its return to the Absolute, and we the Brothers have always fulfilled our duty of warning and teaching. Those who in that remote past in the ancient Earth-Moon rejected the Great Arcanum became terribly wicked lunar demons. Those sublunar demons are now dwelling in the abyss.

A few human beings of the fifth root-race of the Moon accepted the Great Arcanum very late, and now they are rising to the angelic state. That straggling group was given a new dwelling place. That group lives now in another planet.

The brothers Max Heindel and Rudolf Steiner made the mistake of believing that the Moon is a piece of earth projected into space. Those of us who worked in that remote past with the lunar humanity know that the Moon was an earth of space, older than our planet Earth.

175

The Moon is the mother of the Earth, because the life that is now evolving in our planet Earth was in the past incarnated in the Moon.

In those days of the ancient Earth-Moon, when life started its return to the Absolute, then it also experienced its tremendous apocalypse. And now when the great life has absolutely left the earth, then it will become a new Moon too.

The sublunar spheres constitute the abyss.

To mention the name of the Virgin in those dark regions means to provoke the demons' anger.

The adepts of the shadow hate the Virgin, and they furiously attack anyone who dares to mention her name in their regions.

The Virgin Mother of the world is Kundalini.

The adepts of the shadow hate the Great Mother who, as a serpent of fire, ascends along the spinal canal.

When the serpent goes down from the coccyx, it turns into the tail of Satan. The descending serpent is the horrible tempting snake of Eden.

In angels, the serpent ascends victoriously along the spinal canal. In demons, the serpent is the tail of Satan.

CHAPTER 31

The Millennium and
the Judgement

'*And I saw an angel* (the fifth of the seven) *coming down from heaven, holding in his hand the key of the abyss and a great chain.*' (Rev. 20:1).

'*And he seized the dragon, that ancient serpent* (Jahve), *who is the Devil and Satan, and bound him for a thousand years.*' (Rev. 20:2).

In the year 1950, the genie of evil, whose name is Jahve, was thrown into the abyss. Jahve is now paying a terrible Karma. Jahve is a fallen, terribly wicked angel. Jahve is that demon who tempted Jesus in the desert, and as he was tempting him he said to him: *Itababo*. Jahve is the supreme head of the Black Lodge. Jahve is the secret author of the crucifixion of our Adorable Saviour. Jahve is the antithetic pole of Jesus. The Roman soldiers who crucified the Adorable One constitute Jahve's guard of honour. Jahve is now crucified in the abyss. That is his Karma. The cross of the devil is upside down.

Jahve is now crucified with his head down and his feet up. The Jewish people worship Jahve and follow Jahve.

The fifth of the seven '*threw him into the abyss, and shut it and sealed it over him, so that he would deceive the nations no more, until the thousand years were ended. After that he must be loosed for a little while.*' (Rev. 20:3).

Jahve and his legions will remain in the abyss for one age. After that he must be loosed for a little while.

The lost ones will be given one last opportunity so that they can repent.

'And he will be loosed from his prison and will come out to deceive the nations that are at the four corners of the earth, Gog and Magog, to gather them for battle. Their number is like the sand of the sea.' (Rev. 20:8).

'And they marched up over the broad earth and surrounded the camp of the saints and the beloved city, but fire came down out of heaven from God and consumed them.' (Rev. 20:9).

Woe, woe, woe to those wretched who will not be able to seize the last and very brief opportunity that will be given to them, to the lost ones. They will sink into the abyss forever.

'And the devil who had deceived them was thrown into the lake of fire and sulphur where the beast and the false prophet were, and they will be tormented day and night for ever and ever.' (Rev. 20:10).

'And I saw the dead, great and small, standing before the throne, and books (of Karma) *were opened. Also another book was opened, which is the book of life. And the dead were judged according to what was written in the books, according to their works.'* (Rev. 20:12).

Every human being has his own book. The works of every human being are written in this book in sacred characters.

'And the sea gave up the dead that were in it, Death and Hades gave up the dead that were in them, and all were judged according to their works.' (Rev. 20:13).

'Then Death and Hades were thrown into the lake of fire. This is the second death.' (Rev. 20:14).

'And anyone whose name was not found written in the book of life was thrown into the lake of fire.' (Rev. 20:15).

Life has started its return to the Great Light. The times of the end have already come. Millions of human beings, as numerous as the grains of sand of the sea, already have the horns on their foreheads and the fatal mark on their hands. Jahve was bound in the abyss and the multitudes worship him.

'Then I saw thrones, and those seated on them were given authority to judge. I also saw the souls of those who had been beheaded for their testimony to Jesus and for the word of God, and who had not worshipped the beast or its image and had not received its mark on their foreheads or their hands. They came to life and reigned with Christ a thousand years (a great age).' (Rev. 20:4).

Since ancient times, all those who accepted the A.Z.F. Arcanum became kings and priests of nature. They will govern now, in the New Era, under the command of the Christ.

This is the first resurrection. And the kings, the divine kings, will reincarnate to govern.

'Blessed and holy are those who share in the first resurrection. Over these the second death has no power, but they will be priests of God and of Christ, and they will reign with him a thousand years (one age).' (Rev. 20:6).

The second death is exceedingly frightful and terrible. In the abyss the adepts of the shadow disintegrate slowly until they die. That is the second death.

Those who accept the A.Z.F. Arcanum will be saved from the abyss and the second death. They will become gods, and they will sing: Hallelujah! Hallelujah! Hallelujah!

PART THREE

THE NEW JERUSALEM

'SICUT QUAE SUPERIUS SICUT QUOD INFERIUS'

CHAPTER 32

The New Jerusalem

'*A*nd *I saw a new heaven a new earth* (the future earth, after the great cataclysm), *for the first heaven and the first earth* (the present one) *had passed away, and the sea was no more.*' (Rev. 21:1).

'*And I saw the holy city, the new Jerusalem* (the earth of the future sixth race), *coming down out of heaven from God, prepared as a bride adorned for her husband* (the Christ).' (Rev. 21:2).

'*And I heard a loud voice from the throne saying, "Behold, the dwelling of God is with men. He will dwell with them, and they will be his people, and God himself* (the Inner God) *will be with them.*' (Rev. 21:3).

'*"And he will wipe away every tear from their eyes, and death will be no more, neither will be there mourning nor crying nor pain any more, for the former things have passed away."*' (Rev. 21:4).

'*And the one who sat on the throne* (the Inner God) *said, "Behold, I make all things new". Also he said, "Write this, for these words are trustworthy and true."*' (Rev. 21:5).

'*And he said to me, "It is done! I am the Alpha and the Omega, the beginning and the end. To the thirsty I will give from the fountain of the water of life without paying for it."*' (Rev. 21:6). He is indeed the Alpha and the Omega, the beginning and the end of all things.

Man has a body, a soul and an Intimate. Beyond the Intimate, every man has three depths: the first depth is the origin of life; the second depth is the origin of speech, and the third depth is the origin of sexual force.

These three divine depths of every man constitute the shinning Dragon of Wisdom. Every man has his own Dragon of Wisdom. He is the Inner God. And he is the Alpha and the Omega, the beginning and the end. He is the Inner Christ who man needs to incarnate within himself.

To the thirsty he will give from the fountain of the water of life without paying for it. Blessed are those who are able to drink from the pure waters of life, because they will never be thirsty again. (John 4:14).

The key lies in the A.Z.F. Arcanum.

The Fire (I — Ignis) must fertilize the Water (A — Aqua, water) so that the Spirit (O — Origo, beginning, spirit) can be born.

The great Master Huiracocha has spoken about the mantram I.A.O. at length in his book *Logos, Mantram, Magic* and in his *Rosicrucian Novel*. This mantram has to be vocalized word by word, separating every letter and prolonging the sound of every letter, when we are connected to our wife (our priestess). This is how the sacred serpent awakens.

'*He who conquers* (sexual passion) *will inherit these things, and I will be his God* (I will incarnate in him), *and he will be my son* (because he has become christified). *But as for the cowardly, the faithless, the polluted, the murderers, the fornicators, the sorcerers, the idolaters, and all liars, their lot will be in the lake that burns with fire and sulphur, which is the second death.*' (Rev. 21:7-8).

The lake that burns with fire and sulphur is the lake of carnal passion. That lake is man's low animal nature, and its atomic region is the abyss. There the adepts of the shadow disintegrate slowly until they die. That is the second death.

'Then one of the seven angels who had the seven bowls full of the seven last plagues came and spoke to me, saying, "Come, I will show you the Bride, the wife of the Lamb."' (Rev. 21:9).

Human beings can travel in their astral bodies to anywhere in the world or in hell. The key for conscious projection in the astral body is the following: Lying in bed face up, let the disciple fall slightly asleep while vocalizing the syllables LA – RA. The student will vocalize these two syllables separately, one by one, in this way: LA.......RA...... The vocalization of these two sacred syllables is to be done mentally.

These two syllables have the power to make man's sexual energies vibrate intensely. The disciple will calmly fall slightly asleep in bed vocalizing these two syllables. As the student vocalizes them, the sexual energies, the creative energies of the Third Logos, start to vibrate.

When this kind of energy vibrates intensely, it produces a very sweet and calm sound, something similar to the crickets' singing. Students must learn to use this sound. That is the subtle voice that gives us the power to project ourselves consciously in our astral body. When the students hear the mystic sound, they must get out of bed and go to anywhere in the world. It is not a question of getting out of bed mentally. What we are now teaching must be translated into actions.

As the disciples get out of bed, they leave their physical bodies, and then they can go into the higher worlds to study the great mysteries of life and death. If anyone wants to learn how to sing these two sacred syllables, let them listen to Mozart's Magic Flute. That work was an initiation which Mozart received in Egypt.

The prophet was taken out of his body in the spirit and was carried away to be shown the Heavenly Jerusalem. *'And in the spirit he carried me away to a great, high mountain, and showed me the holy city Jerusalem coming down out of heaven from God, having the glory of God, and its radiance was like a most rare jewel, like jasper, clear as crystal.'* (Rev. 21:10-11).

185

This very precious stone, like jasper, symbolizes the sexual organs of the christified masters. The stone is clear as crystal. Let us remember the crystal: the liquid, flexible and malleable glass. That glass is the christonic semen: V.I.T.R.I.O.L. (*Visita Interiora Terrae Rectificando Invenies Occultum Lapidem* — Visit the interior of the earth and by rectifying you will find the occult stone). That occult stone is the philosopher's stone. We have to search in the interior of our philosophical earth, and by rectifying we will find that very precious stone, like jasper, clear as crystal.

Inmissium Membri Virilis in Vagina Feminae sine Ejaculatio Seminis.

The wise Huiracocha says, '*Try it. The position that has been described can be kept for an hour, and a sensation of ineffable well-being will be felt. A chest against the other chest, the two solar plexuses in close contact, all the astral centres put together one on top of the other, this allows for an exchange of currents of energy to establish a right androgyny.*'

Every initiate builds his own Jerusalem on the living stone. That stone is sex. There exists the Jerusalem in man, the Jerusalem above and the Jerusalem below. *Sicut quae superius sicut quod inferius.*

The higher worlds are the Jerusalem above. The earth of the future sixth race is the Jerusalem below. Man and all his christified vehicles are the human Jerusalem. The New Jerusalem shines full of glory.

'*It had a great, high wall with twelve gates* (the twelve zodiacal gates in the universe and in man), *and at the gates twelve* (zodiacal) *angels, and on the gates the names of the twelve tribes of the sons of Israel were inscribed.*' (Rev. 21:12). They are the twelve fundamental types in which humanity is divided in accordance with the influence of the twelve zodiacal signs.

As above, so below. Man has twelve faculties which are governed by twelve atomic angels. In starry space and in man there are twelve zodiacal signs. It is necessary to transmute the sexual energy and make it go through the twelve zodiacal gates of the human organism.

The prophet goes on to speak about the twelve zodiacal gates in this way: *'On the east three gates, on the north three gates, on the south three gates, and on the west three gates.'* (Rev. 21:13).

'And the wall of the city had twelve foundations, and on them are the twelve names of the twelve apostles of the Lamb.' (Rev. 21:14). The twelve zodiacal signs and the twelve spheres of energy that penetrate and compenetrate one another without becoming confused.

Solar humanity becomes completely realized in the twelve planes. The Arcanum Twelve is the foundation of the Heavenly Jerusalem. The Arcanum Twelve is the symbol of sexual alchemy. The Arcanum Twelve is shown in the Tarot in this way: *Symbol: a man who is hanging from one of his feet, and whose hands are tied at his back, so that his body is forming a triangle with its main point pointing down and his legs are forming a cross above the triangle. The potence is like a Hebrew Taw in shape. The two trees that support the potence have each six cut branches.* This is the sacrifice and the work completed. This is called sexual alchemy.

There are in the world millions of books on Yoga, Occultism, Theosophy, Rosicrucianism, etc. There are also thousands of schools, some of them with very ancient, venerable traditions.

A student might subject himself to the most rigorous disciplines, practise the Kriya, visit thousands of schools, centres, lodges, acquire certificates and degrees, and receive beautiful, very resounding names from his instructors, but if the student does not practise sexual magic, he may be very venerable to his own people, he may be a very educated and even a learned person.

But up there, in the higher worlds, he will be always considered a person just keen on spiritual studies, an ignorant disciple, a poor mystic shadow, a profane, or at worst a dangerous individual. We have to work with the Gold and the Silver. We have to work with the Moon and the Sun in order to build the Heavenly Jerusalem within ourselves. The Gold and the Silver, the Sun and the Moon, are the sexual forces of man and woman.

Women alchemists must not reach physiological orgasm either. In that way they can transmute their sexual energies and awaken the snake. The highest degree which woman can reach in these studies is the degree of Virgin.

Sexual alchemy is the Hermetic Art. The Hermetic Art is highly scientific, highly philosophical and highly mystical. In the Arcanum Twelve is contained the whole science and philosophy of the Great Work. In the christonic semen lies the living and philosophical secret fire. The mysticism of sexual alchemy is the mysticism of all the old initiates.

The philosophy of sexual alchemy has its principles in the school of the Essenes, in the school of Alexandria, in the teachings of Pythagoras, in the mysteries of Egypt, Troy, Rome, Carthage, Eleusis, in the wisdom of the Aztecs and Mayas, etc.

The science of sexual alchemy and its methods must be studied in the books of Paracelsus, Nicholas Flamel, Raymond Lully. We also find these methods hidden amidst the veil of all symbols, in the hieratic figures of the old hieroglyphics of many ancient temples, in the Greek and Egyptian myths, etc.

You who are seeking Initiation, you who are reading so many books, you who are all the time flitting from school to school, always searching, always longing, always yearning, tell me honestly: Have you already awakened your Kundalini? Have you already opened the seven churches of your spinal cord? Have you already incarnated the Lamb?

You who are seeking, tell me: Can you already control earthquakes? Can you walk on water? Can you control hurricanes? Can you calm storms? Can you speak in the Golden Language? Can you see in the higher worlds, and can you study the whole history of the earth and its races in the sealed archives of nature?

Answer me, brother reader. Be honest to yourself. Put your hand on your heart and answer me honestly: Have you become realized? Are you certain that with your theories you will become a god? What have you attained? What have you achieved with all your theories?

The poor servant who is writing this book is an initiate into the Lemurian, Egyptian, Tibetan, etc. Mysteries, and in the history of the ages he never knew any genuine master who had been able to become christified without practising sexual magic.

If you hope to become liberated, to become realized, to become christified without practising sexual magic, you are to be pitied, you deserve compassion, you are an imbecile.

The lead of the personality has to be transmuted into the most pure gold of the spirit.

The salt (matter) and the sulphur (fire) are urgent in order to prepare the philosophical mercury (semen). This mercury has to be transmuted and sublimated to the heart. The Christ is in the heart. The forces coming from above mix in the heart with the forces coming up from below. What is below must mix with what is above, so that what is below can ascend to the higher worlds of the Great Light.

That is how we succeed in uniting the cross with the triangle. Cross-man must be linked to the triangle-spirit through the potable gold (the sacred fire of sex). These are the twelve foundations of the Heavenly Jerusalem.

The man who forms in his mother's womb is the result of the sexual act. He is not the result of any theory or any school. Man is a child of a male and of a female. There were kisses, there was love, there was a man, there was a woman and there was also a sexual intercourse that engendered you and that mother who gave birth to you.

Why are you forgetting that? What theory did they engender you with? Why do you want to be born now as a Master of the Great Day in the worlds of the Light excluding the Phallus and the Womb? What is natural is natural, dear reader. Do not make the mistake of wanting to be born through theories. No one can be born through the legs, or to eat with the knees. Every thing in its own place. Every thing with its own thing.

What is natural is natural. The birth of the Son of Man is a hundred per cent sexual. If, despite all that we are saying to you, you still have hopes to attain Initiation by practising the famous bellows system — only through practising breathing exercises. Time and years will prove to you that you are wrong, and you will tumble down into the abyss inevitably.

Bellows systems, asanas, kriyas, etc. are all magnificent; they are wonderful. We cannot underestimate them. They are useful helpers for the awakening of the chakras and the cleansing of the nervous canals, etc. But if the yogi does not practise sexual magic, he will sink into the abyss, although he is a fanatic practitioner of the bellows system.

'And the one who talked to me had a measuring rod of gold to measure the city and its gates and walls.' (Rev. 21:15). The rod of gold symbolizes man's spine.

The spinal fires ascend along the spinal cord. The development, ascent and evolution of Kundalini is extremely difficult. Every one of the thirty-three spinal vertebras corresponds to the thirty-three sacred chambers of the temple. The spinal fires are controlled by the fires of the heart. Kundalini ascends very slowly by means of sexual magic and sanctification. Each vertebra has its own virtues and trials. It is impossible to achieve the ascent to any vertebra without the permission of the cardiac fires. The merits of the heart control the ascent of Kundalini.

The guru who has not received the rod is not a true guru. Every initiate who raises the serpent on the rod receives the cane. The city and its gates and its walls must be measured with the rod. The Jerusalem of every man must be measured with the rod. The master who still has not awakened his Kundalini is a false prophet.

There are Three Halls. The First Hall is the hall of ignorance. The Second Hall is the hall of study. The Third Hall is the hall of wisdom.

The human multitudes live in the First Hall. In the Second Hall are found all the theories, schools, lodges, orders, etc. The Third Hall is the hall of wisdom. In this hall we find the Master and the Inner God who lead us to the Great Light.

When we are in the Second Hall, we study Astrology, Yogism, Theosophy, etc.

We are then searching. We visit schools. We flit from flower to flower. Every flower is a sect, theory, school, lodge, etc. Thus, there are people who spend many reincarnations searching, nosing here and there, reading, etc.

When the student gets tired of longing and finally wants to know, he walks in through the narrow and difficult door. That door is sex. Then it is when we really are in the Third Hall — the Hall of Wisdom. In this hall we find the Inner God and the Guru who lead us to the Great Reality. We need to build the Heavenly Jerusalem on the living stone.

'And the city lies foursquare, its length the same as its width; and he measured the city with his rod, twelve thousand stadia; its length and width and height are equal.' (Rev. 21:16).

We have arrived at the quadrature of the circle, at the perpetual movement. The city lies foursquare. This reminds us of the Holy and Mysterious Tetragrammaton, the Holy Four.

If we fully explore the interior of our Divine Being, we can find three depths. Those three depths emanate from the mathematical point. It is urgent to know that that point is a superdivine atom of the Absolute Abstract Space. The kabbalistic name for that atom is Ain Soph.

The three christic depths within us emanate from Ain Soph. This is the ternary that has emanated from the mathematical point. $3 + 1 = 4$. Three plus one equals four. This is the Holy Tetragrammaton.

The Dragon of Wisdom (the Inner Christ) emanated from Ain Soph, and will return to Ain Soph. The city lies foursquare because it is the perfect temple of the Lamb. And he measured the city with the rod, twelve thousand stadia. The number twelve thousand is kabbalistically broken down in this way: 12,000 = 1 + 2 = 3. Here we have the ternary, the Lamb who emanated from a superdivine atom.

The Adorable One shines within the inner vehicles of all who have become christified. That is love.

It is impossible to build the New Jerusalem without the Holy Four.

The name of the Eternal has four Hebraic letters: IOD, HE, VAU, HE.

These are the four winds. Few are those who know how to pronounce this name as it should be pronounced. Whoever wants to build the New Jerusalem must awaken the sacred fire of Kundalini. The pentecostal serpent is INRI, the Azoth. The sun is its father. The moon is its mother. The wind bore it in its womb. And the philosophical earth was its wet nurse.

The alchemist who wants to build the New Jerusalem must work in his laboratory with the sulphur (fire), the azoth (air), the mercury (water) and the earth.

The Great Work is symbolized by the lion (fire), the eagle (air), the man (water) and the bull (earth).

These four elements form the Cross of Initiation. Know you that the Cross of Initiation is received in the Temple-Heart.

We must work with the elementals of fire, of air, of waters and of earth in the Sacred Mountain. That Sacred Mountain, whether it is the Himalayas or the Alps or the Andean Mountain Range, symbolizes the spinal cord with its thirty-three vertebras. In the Sacred Mountain we must be alchemists. Only in that way can we receive the initiation in our Temple-Heart. We need to transmute the lead into gold in order to build the New Jerusalem.

The salamanders kindle the fire and fertilize the undines of water so that life can come into existence.

The gnomes or pigmies, who dwell in the Great Mountain Range, transmute the lead into gold. The joyful and playful sylphs liven up the fire so that the Great Work can be performed.

The container must be hermetically closed to prevent, at all costs, the *Prima Materia* from spilling. That is how the lead of the personality is transmuted into the living gold of the spirit.

The container must be livened up by the fire of the salamanders. '*Coct again and again, and do not tire of cocting.*'

The sylphs of air liven up the flames of your thought. The gnomes will transmute the lead of your passions into the gold of the spirit, and the undines, at times passionate, will move full of joy in the *Prima Materia* or Universal Sperm.

The creatures of fire, of air, of water and of earth cannot be absent from the Great Work. Without the creatures of the four elements, the lead cannot be transmuted into gold.

The gnomes could not transmute the lead into gold without water and without undines. The water and the undines must be fertilized and warmed by the burning fire of the salamanders. Only in that way is it possible to evaporate the waters and to transmute the lead of the personality into the most pure gold of the spirit. Without the mystic action of the sylphs, the alchemist loses heart and the Great Work fails. These creatures of the four elements are within ourselves, here and now. Every master of metallic transmutations builds the Heavenly Jerusalem.

'*And the city lies foursquare, its length the same as its width.*' Without the Holy Four, it is impossible to build the New Jerusalem.

Iod is man. *He* is woman. *Vau* is the phallus. *He* is the vulva.

The ineffable things are written with the Holy Name of the Eternal. And the four living creatures come and go. The four sacred letters move and combine in the whole of creation.

'*And he also measured its wall, one hundred and forty-four cubits, by a man's measure, that is, an angel's.*' (Rev. 21:17). 144 = 1 + 4 + 4 = 9. This is the Ninth Sphere (sex). We have to go down to the Ninth Sphere (sex) and work with the fire and water, origin of worlds, beasts, men and gods. Every genuine white initiation begins there.

All those who incarnated him — Hermes, Jesus, Krishna, Rama, etc. — went down to the Ninth Sphere. Also Buddha, Dante, Pythagoras, etc. went down to the Ninth Sphere.

Hillarius IX says that in the ancient mysteries the descent to the Ninth Sphere was the greatest test for the supreme dignity of the Hierophant.

Nine is man's measure, that is, an angel's. We remain in our mother's womb for nine months. Only in the Ninth Sphere can the Son of Man be born. No angel has ever been known who is not born in the Ninth Sphere.

Whoever wants to cut the head of Medusa (the I) must go down to the Ninth Sphere.

Whoever wants to incarnate the Christ has to go down to the Ninth Sphere. Whoever wants to dissolve the I must go down to the Ninth Sphere. The Ninth Sphere is the *Sanctum Regnum* of the divine omnipotence of the Third Logos. In the Ninth Sphere we find the Forge of Vulcan.

Every squab who is working in the Great Work must lean on his own staff, illuminate himself with his own lamp and wrap himself in his own sacred mantle. Every squab must be prudent. If you want to incarnate the Christ, be like lemon. Keep away from lust and alcohol. Kill even the innermost roots of desire.

'*And the wall was built of jasper, while the city was pure gold, clear as glass.*' (Rev. 21:18). Only with the philosopher's stone (sex) can we build the wall of the New Jerusalem. While the city (man's inner vehicles) was pure gold, clear as glass. The lions of gold adorn the thrones of the divine kings. Gold symbolizes the sexual fire of Kundalini.

Potable gold (pentecostal fire) is similar to the flexible and malleable liquid glass. That glass is the christonic semen. The dorsal fires are pentecostal. The fires of the heart are christic, and the rays of the Father sparkle terribly on the forehead.

'And the foundations of the wall of the city were adorned with every jewel. The first was jasper (the philosopher's stone), *the second sapphire, the third agate, the fourth emerald, the fifth onyx, the sixth carnelian, the seventh chrysolite, the eighth beryl, the ninth topaz, the tenth chrysoprase, the eleventh jacinth, the twelve amethyst.'* (Rev. 21:19-20). Each one of these stones represents some specific virtues. All these sacred stones adorn the sword of justice.

There are nine initiations of lesser mysteries and seven great portals of greater mysteries. The Intimate is the one receiving all initiations. The Testament of Wisdom says, *'Before the false dayspring dawned upon the earth, those who survived the hurricane and the storm praised the Intimate, and the Heralds of the Dayspring appeared to them.'*

The I receives no initiations. The human personality receives nothing. Yet the I of many initiates becomes filled with pride, saying, 'I am a master. I have such and such initiations.' The I thinks that it is an initiate and enjoys reincarnating to become perfect, or so it says. The I never becomes perfect. The I reincarnates to satisfy its desires. That is all.

The experiences of every reincarnation make the I more and more complicated, turning it more and more wicked. Evolution is a process of complication of life. As we gradually dissolve the I, we receive the precious stones. In the higher worlds the Intimate receives his sacred stones: rings, chains, ineffable jewels adorned with the sacred stones, etc.

Any bad action is enough for the initiate to lose certain sacred stones, which means loss of degrees. An initiate who forced his wife to perform the sexual act when she was ill was about to lose a sapphire of his sword. Fortunately the initiate obeyed when he was warned by the White Lodge.

The I is memory, a bunch of memories, dust of the ages. As we dissolve it, we receive degrees and very precious stones.

When the Dragon of Wisdom has dissolved the I, then the Ten Sephiroth shine like precious stones in his ineffable body of glory.

We must first decapitate the I with the sword in the Forge of Vulcan. After that we begin to die slowly. The I dissolves gradually through Alchemy and rigorous understanding. That is total revolution.

'And the twelve gates were twelve pearls, each of the gates made of a single pearl, and the street of the city was pure gold, transparent as glass.' (Rev. 21:21).

Pearls are lunar. Sex is lunar. The twelve pearls symbolize the sexual fire of Pentecost shining in the twelve faculties of man. The street of the Heavenly Jerusalem is pure gold, transparent as glass. The human Jerusalem has twelve gates, that is, twelve vehicles.

The Theosophist brothers have studied man's septenary. Every christified master has twelve bodies, that is, twelve vehicles which connect him to the Great Reality. There are twelve spheres of energy where a solar humanity lives and unfolds. And the Heavenly Jerusalem has therefore twelve gates, and each gate is a pearl, a region or a world.

There exists also a Zodiacal Belt with twelve constellations. The New Jerusalem — the earth of the future sixth race — is being gestated in the zodiacal womb. Every evolution begins in Leo and ends in Leo.

The street of the city is pure gold (sacred fire), like the flexible and malleable glass, also called christonic semen. The pentecostal fire rises from that liquid glass. All the twelve vehicles of a christified master shine gloriously amidst the fire and the light of infinite space. Those are the twelve pearls. That is the Heavenly Jerusalem.

Every inhabitant of the New Jerusalem will be, by himself, a true Heavenly Jerusalem.

'*And I saw no temple in the city, for its temple is the Lord God the Almighty* (the Inner Being) *and the Lamb.*' (Rev. 21:22).

This verse does not mean that the cosmic temples of inner instruction will cease to exist. It is a deeper question. In the New Jerusalem the seven present religions and the five thousand sects will have no reason to exist, because the Lamb will be incarnated in every man. That will be the age of the Christ.

'*And the city has no need of* (physical) *sun or* (physical) *moon to shine on it, for the glory of God is its light, and its lamp is the Lamb.*' (Rev. 21:23).

'*And the nations will walk by its light, and the kings of the earth* (initiates) *will bring their glory into it.*' (Rev. 21:24).

'*And its gates will never be shut by day — and there will be no night there.*' (Rev. 21:25).

'*And they will bring into it the glory and the honour of the nations.*' (Rev. 21:26).

'*But nothing unclean will enter it, nor anyone who practise abomination or falsehood, but only those who are written in the book of life of the Lamb.*' (Rev. 21:27).

Chapter 33

The River of the Water of Life

It is necessary that the students of the Great World Gnostic Movement (AGLA) receive Initiation.

Imagination, inspiration and intuition are the three compulsory pathways to Initiation.

Our thoughts, feelings and will must be set completely free from our physical body.

It is essential that we learn to project ourselves consciously in our astral body.

First. The Gnostic student will rise to imaginative knowledge.

Second. The student will acquire inspirative knowledge.

Third. The student will obtain intuitive knowledge.

The student will train with imagination for some time, then with inspiration, and later with intuition.

PRACTICES

1. Imaginative Knowledge

The syllables MA-MA, PA-PA, BA-BA are the first syllables we articulate when we are children. With these syllables you can begin Initiation. Sing them adopting an infantile, innocent attitude. In Mozart's Magic Flute you can learn the intonation of those sacred syllables. Mozart put those syllables in his marvellous work.

Fall slightly asleep adopting an infantile attitude, remembering the first years of your childhood and intoning the sacred syllables mentally.

The word *papa* is vocalized intoning the first syllable PA on a high pitch, and then lowering the pitch in the second syllable PA. Then you will articulate the syllable PA many times. You will do the same with the syllable MA.

Fall slightly asleep meditating on your childhood. Relive your whole childhood with your imagination. Articulate the sacred syllables mentally.

Know that every child is clairvoyant until the age of four years. After that age, the innocent atoms of clairvoyance plunge into the subconscious. If you want to reconquer the faculty of clairvoyance, meditate on your childhood and fall slightly and deeply asleep articulating the child's first syllables: MA, MA, PA, PA, BA, BA.

Meditation and the sacred syllables will awaken the infantile atoms of clairvoyance. Then you will rise to imaginative knowledge. You will learn to think in living images. The present race only thinks in concepts of ideas. Ideas are the result of desire.

Someone thinks of winning the heart of a woman, then he is struck by an idea, and so on. Ideas come from the I. You will learn to think with living images. Infantile meditation and the sacred syllables will awaken your infantile atoms to a new activity.

Imaginative knowledge gives you the power to travel in your etheric body consciously and positively. When the student has attained imaginative knowledge, then he or she can begin the exercises for inspirative knowledge.

2. Inspirative Knowledge

We have given many keys for conscious astral projection, and thousands of students have learned to project themselves in their astral bodies.

However, we have seen in practice that those people who cannot keep their minds quiet even for an instant, those who are used to flitting from school to school, from lodge to lodge, always uneasy, always worried, they are not able to project themselves consciously in their astral bodies.

The key for conscious projection in the astral body is to empty the mind.

Lying in bed, the student will beg his Inner God to take him out of the body. Then, after having prayed, the student must empty his mind. For this practice it is useless to think.

Having understood the uselessness of thinking, the student will not think absolutely of anything. Thus, understanding the uselessness of thinking, the mind will become quiet and silent during this practice.

First of all we must understand that the process of thinking is an obstacle for us to project consciously in our astral body.

When we understand the uselessness of thinking during this practice which leads us to inspired knowledge, then the mind becomes quiet and silent naturally.

We have to distinguish between a mind that is quiet and a mind that is quietened.

We have to distinguish between a mind that is silent and a mind that is forced to be silent.

When the mind is quietened and silenced violently, then there is a secret struggle, and consequently the mind is not quiet or silent.

When we have understood the uselessness of thinking during these practices, then the mind becomes quiet and silent by itself.

Next let the student go calmly to sleep. If the student manages to go to sleep without thinking, with his mind quiet and silent, then he will awaken consciously outside his physical body and will rise to inspired knowledge.

It is essential for the dreamer to awaken. The awakening of consciousness is urgent. All the human beings travel in their astral bodies during the sleeping hours, but unfortunately they are in the astral plane with their consciousness asleep; they go around dreaming.

When the dreamer awakens from his dreams, he rises to inspired knowledge. The Masters of the White Lodge do not dream. Their consciousness is continuously awake and in a state of watchfulness, although their physical bodies are asleep in bed.

3. Intuitive Knowledge.

The third phase of knowledge is intuitive knowledge. In order to reach the ineffable summits of intuitive knowledge we have to kiss our tormentor's whip and the hand of the one who beats us.

We must love and adore the whole of humanity, sacrifice ourselves for humanity and be always ready to give even the last drop of our blood for the sake of that poor suffering humanity.

When initiates move consciously in their astral bodies, they can induce the state of ecstasy on themselves through love. Initiates then leave their astral bodies and rise to the worlds of angels, archangels, seraphs, powers, virtues, thrones, etc.

It is then when we rise to intuitive knowledge.

Whoever reaches the ineffable summits of intuition can see the future Heavenly Jerusalem.

Those who go up the three steps of imagination, inspiration and intuition can see the old Jerusalem (the old earth) and the future Jerusalem (the future earth that comes after the great cataclysm).

'And I saw a new heaven and a new earth, for the first heaven and the first earth had passed away, and the sea was no more.'

(Rev 21:1). The inhabitants of the future earth will be citizens who will be awake in the higher worlds. In the future Jerusalem there will be only happiness, peace and love.

'Then he showed me the river of the water of life, bright as crystal, flowing from the throne of God and of the Lamb.' (Rev. 22:1).

That river of the water of eternal life is the christonic semen. Those who long to go up the three steps of imagination, inspiration and intuition must wash their errors in the pure water of life.

Without chastity no progress is attained in these studies.

'Through the middle of the street of the city and on either side of the river was the tree of life (with its Ten Sephiroth), *with its twelve kinds of fruit* (the twelve faculties), *yielding its fruit each month, and the leaves of the tree were for the healing of the nations.'* (Rev. 22:2). Then no one will make a bad use of their powers.

All those who have gone up the three steps of imagination, inspiration and intuition can move consciously in their inner vehicles and visit the higher worlds. The Ten Sephiroth constitute the ten atomic waves of the Great Universal Life.

The initiate knows how to move consciously through the ten waves of life.

There is a secret sephiroth. That secret sephiroth is the Ain Soph (the world of the Absolute Abstract Space). The fatal antithesis of the Ain Soph is the abyss.

Initiates who make a bad use of their twelve faculties become black magicians and fall into the abyss.

In the New Jerusalem, the leaves and the fruits of the tree of life will be for the healing of the nations.

'Nothing accursed will be found there any more, but the throne of God and of the Lamb will be in it, and his servants will worship him.' (Rev. 22:3).

'And they will see his face, and his name will be on their fore-heads.' (Rev. 22:4).

All those who receive the name of the Eternal on their fore-heads have been saved from the abyss and from the second death.

No sceptic, no faithless man, can enter the New Jerusalem. It is better for those who doubt to make ready to enter the abyss. Those who ejaculate the semen, the sorcerers, murderers, liars... are all people of the abyss. Those people cannot receive the name of God on their foreheads.

Only people full of faith, love, chastity and charity will live in the New Jerusalem.

'And there will be no more night. They need no light of lamp or (physical) *sun, for the* (Inner) *Lord God will be their light, and they will reign for ever and ever.'* (Rev. 22:5).

'And he said to me, "These words are trustworthy and true. And the Lord, the God of the spirits of the prophets, has sent his angel to show his servants what must soon take place.' (Rev. 22:6).

All those who have gone up the steps of imagination, inspi-ration and intuition are awake in the higher worlds. When an initiate is outside his physical body, he can ask his Master to show him the future Jerusalem and what must soon take place. What is needed here is to give up laziness and to do the prac-tices of imagination, inspiration and intuition, which will lead us to Initiation.

'"And behold, I am coming soon!" Blessed is the one who keeps the words of the prophecy of this book. (Rev. 22:7).

This is the Message of Aquarius. This is the book of the New Era.

This is the Secret Doctrine of the Saviour of the world.

The Seer of Revelation (who, incidentally, is now disincar-nated) goes on to say the following, *'I John am he who heard and saw these things. And when I heard and saw them, I fell down to worship at the feet of the angel who showed them to me.'* (Rev. 22:8).

'But he said to me, "You must not do that! I am a fellow servant with you and your brothers the prophets, and with those who keep the words of this book. Worship God."' (Rev. 22:9).

The angel did not want to be worshipped. Yet thousands of disciples enjoy being worshipped by people. These are the ones who say, 'I am a great clairvoyant, nothing is hidden from me. I know everything. I am a great initiate. I am a Master...'

Satan enjoys praising himself. The psychological I is Satan. Satan is the one who says, 'I am the reincarnation of a great Master, or of a great man.'

A truly humble bodhisattva never praises himself. The humble bodhisattva says, 'I am a miserable worm of the mud of the earth. I am a man like any other man. I am worthless. The work is everything.'

The bodhisattva is the human soul of the Master. The Master is the Inner God.

The Milky Way Temple is marvellous. A big stone prevents the profane from going in. Inside that temple we find thousands of bodhisattvas of the Milky Way. They look like humble illiterate peasants. Nevertheless, the Inner God of every one of them governs constellations and worlds.

When we throw ourselves at the feet of those humble men to worship them, they say, 'I am nobody. I know nothing. I am worthless.'

'You must not do that! I am a fellow servant with you and your brothers the prophets.'

Man in himself is a sinful shadow. Only the Seer of the Seer, the Father who is in secret, is perfect.

'And he said to me, "Do not seal up the words of the prophecy of this book, for the time is near.' (Rev. 22:10).

In the days of John it was still possible to say: '"*Let the evil-doer still do evil, and the filthy still be filthy, and the righteous still do right, and the holy still be holy.*"' (Rev. 22:11).

Now it is not possible to say that, because the times of the end have already come.

This is the moment when we have to define ourselves either as eagles or as reptiles, either as angels or as demons.

'*Behold, I am coming soon, my reward is with me, to repay everyone according to his work.*' (Rev. 22:12).

'*I* (the Lamb) *am the Alpha and the Omega, the first and the last, the beginning and the end.*' (Rev. 22:13).

The Lamb is the Alpha and the Omega, the beginning and the end, the first and the last.

The Well-Beloved One enters the soul to repay everyone according to his work.

'*Blessed are those who do his commandments, so that their power may be in the tree of life* (the Ten Sephiroth), *and may enter the city* (the New Jerusalem) *by the gates* (of sex).' (Rev. 22:14).

'*Outside are the dogs* (the false prophets, those who found bad schools to exploit the souls, the fornicators, etc.) *and sorcerers and fornicators and murderers and idolaters, and everyone who loves and practises falsehood.*' (Rev. 22:15).

'*I Jesus have sent my angel to you with this testimony for the churches.*' And exclaims Jesus, the one who received the Venusta Initiation, saying, '*I am the root and the offspring of David, the bright morning star.*' (Rev. 22:16).

Christ is the star of dawn. Christ enters the soul when the soul receives the Venusta Initiation.

'*And the Spirit* (the Christ) *and the Bride* (the soul) *say, "Come." Let everyone who hears say, "Come." And let everyone who is thirsty come. Let anyone who wishes take the water of life without price.*' (Rev. 22:17).

206

Only by drinking of the water of life will you attain the Venusta Initiation. Those who drink of that pure water of life will never be thirsty again.

We mean by that the following: Those who work with the A.Z.F. Arcanum will raise the Son of Man up within themselves, and then they will never be thirsty again.

'I warn everyone who hears the words of the prophecy of this book: if anyone adds to them, God will add to him the plagues described in this book.' (Rev. 22:18).

'And if anyone takes away from the words of the book of this prophecy, God will take away his share in the tree of life and in the holy city, which are described in this book.' (Rev. 22:19).

All those who want to reproduce this book are free to do so.* All those who, out of a false sense of decency, take the secrets of the A.Z.F. Arcanum away from this book, woe to them! God will take their share away from the Book of Life and from the Holy City, which are described in this book.

You can reproduce this book in order for the Message of Aquarius to reach all the peoples of the earth, but woe! woe! woe! to those who add to it or take the words of the book of this prophecy away from it, because in truth, in truth I say to you, that God will add to them the plagues described in this book.

'The one who testifies to these things says, "Surely I am coming soon." Amen. Come, Lord Jesus!' (Rev. 22:20).

'The grace of our Lord Jesus Christ be with all of you. Amen.' (Rev. 22:21).

*PUBLISHER'S NOTE

It should be stated that in the present book legislation there is no precedent allowing an author to make an *erga omnes* authorization, that is, an authorization in favour of the whole world, for the publication of his or her work. (That would be the same as giving away one's house or one's car in favour of the whole world). Quite the opposite, International Copyright Treaties stress that the publishing contract must be arranged in favour of a *specifically stated person*, that is, the Publisher. Likewise, legislation is categorical in affirming that **copyright cession will take effect only when it is done in favour of a specific person**, and when the rights to be ceded are clearly specified and not only the law articles containing them. For these reasons, the authorization made by the author in this book takes no legal effect. In addition, Samael Aun Weor gave up making this and other similar generic authorizations. We repeat: They do not take any legal effects, and he explained that it was just another esoteric test for his pupils, which some have not been able to pass. Just as many still persist in the idea of vegetarianism, despite the fact that Samael Aun Weor gave it up, so some persist in publishing his work illegally. On the other hand, **his rightful successors have revoked any authorization granted in such generic and vague terms**, because they take no legal effects, and because, in the present framework of the International Conventions and Treaties on Copyright, we readers and publishers must respect and preserve the work of Samael Aun Weor and the rights of his heirs or assignees.

*Arnolda Garro
de Gómez
(V. M. Litelantes)*

Wife and esoteric collaborator of V.M. Samael Aun Weor. After her husband's disincarnation she was entrusted with leading the Gnostic Institutions, and furthermore she carried out, with admirable authority, the task of preserving intact the written and spoken teaching of V. M. Samael Aun Weor, an assignment which she fulfilled until her passing on 5th February 1998.

May this be a token of gratitude from all the students and sympathizers of contemporary Gnosticism, thus recognizing the enormous spiritual level of Mistress Litelantes.

TO THE READER

If after having read this work you are interested in these esoteric studies, you may find interesting to know that there is
a philanthropic institution devoted to the study of Gnostic
Wisdom and the Teaching of Master Samael Aun Weor:

THE GNOSTIC INSTITUTE OF ANTHROPOLOGY
(G.I.A.)

This institution can be contacted by writing to any of the
following addresses:

FOR MORE
GNOSTIC BOOKS
VISIT
GNOSTICEDITIONS.COM